Withdrawn

STAGE WRITING

A PRACTICAL GUIDE

P9-CQA-787

STAGE WRITING

Val Taylor

The Crowood Press

First published in 2002 by
The Crowood Press Ltd
Ramsbury, Marlborough
Wiltshire SN8 2HR

British Library Cataloguing-in-Publication Data
A catalogue record for this book is available from the British Library.

ISBN 1 86126 452 6

Dedication
For Jay, with love.

Acknowledgements
Thanks are due to:
Ashif Verjee, for the text photographs, and for his help and assistance; and to the people who appear in the photographs.

Treva Reimer, for permission to use production photographs for the book's covers.

Jack Davenport and Neil Bartlett, for discussion of *The Servant*.

Methuen Publishing Limited for permission to quote from:
Top Girls by Caryl Churchill (from *Caryl Churchill Plays 2*)
The Beauty Queen of Leenane by Martin McDonagh (from *Martin McDonagh Plays 1*)
and *Blue/Orange* by Joe Penhall.

My colleagues in the Drama Sector, and the School of English and American Studies at the University of East Anglia, for help and support with this project.

Helen Winning, for invaluable support and encouragement throughout.

Typeset by Jean Cussons Typesetting, Diss, Norfolk

Printed and bound in Great Britain by JW Arrowsmith, Bristol

CONTENTS

CONTENTS

CONTENTS

INTRODUCTION

Why do you want to write a theatre play? As opposed to a novel, a short story or a poem? Don't read any further at this point. Take a moment or two and a blank page of a notebook, and write down your first responses to that question. When you have done so, read on, but keep these first thoughts by you. Keep them close by all the time you are working through this book, and while you are writing.

It's rather a good question to begin with, isn't it? It goes to the heart of what you think a play actually is and what, or who, it's for; what the playwright's role is, where that role begins and ends, who else might have a role, what the relationship between their role and yours could (or should) be. It's a question I would like you to keep coming back to throughout your writing process, and it's likely your answer will change and develop as we progress together. Talk back to me, and to yourself, as we go, through the pages of your notebook; it could be in diary form (*'Haven't a clue about ballroom dancing. Why have I got two people dancing? Note: go and ask somebody what the* Paso Doble *looks like.'*); or perhaps in letter form (*'I think you're completely wrong, it's not that, it's this.'*)

As a director, I always keep a rehearsal diary, and there's usually a point, mid-way through the rehearsal period, when I start wailing (privately) about not having a clue what to do next with a scene. (Not good to do that publicly, in front of the actors!) I use the diary to talk it through. It creates a *dialogic* relationship

---

'Letters to George'

When theatre director Max Stafford-Clark staged *The Recruiting Officer* at the Royal Court Theatre – a play written in 1706 by George Farquhar – it frustrated him that the playwright was no longer available to answer questions about what he'd written (Stafford-Clark is a renowned director of new plays, used to having the playwright present during rehearsals). So he wrote a series of *Letters to George*, asking (and trying to answer) the questions he would have asked George Farquhar if he had been available. Those letters are in print now; you might like to read them, and you'll see that it's not such a daft idea as it might sound.

---

between my creative ideas and my critical observation and judgement. Keeping a writing diary might help you, too; it encourages you to think things out, to pin them down. An idea can look quite different on the page from the way it appeared in your mind's eye; and it is this essential, continuous process of transfer from the inside of your head to the two dimensions of the page, and from there to the four dimensions of the stage itself (three of space plus time), with which you and I will always concern ourselves. So using a notebook to write things out, as well as being a means of problem-solving, is also good practice – a little like developing your muscles in sport. Carry your notebook with you, to jot down ideas, observations, scraps of dialogue and questions, whenever they occur to you.

USING THIS BOOK

A play isn't a fixed entity – a thing. Like writing itself, a play is a process, a series of transactions and interactions between various groups of people. And because it is always, in that sense, moving, a play is alive, organic. Think of the process of writing a play as growing it, rather than manufacturing it; 'manufacture' suggests that you are working from a blueprint, design, or formula. Happily, there isn't one, and this book isn't going to offer you one.

What I am going to offer you is a series of ways of thinking about components of your play; a mesh of approaches for you to try out, or disagree with, shout at, ignore, change and rework as best suits you and the plays you want to write. My suggestions won't necessarily work for everyone, or for every play. But I hope they will get you going – having something to push against can be stimulating!

There are two kinds of exercises in this book: some are questions to be thought about, whilst others are scriptwriting exercises. Both kinds are followed by my comments. Try the exercise first before reading the comments; it will give you greater freedom. For those of you who are already writing, some exercises may seem too familiar, unnecessary, or even (possibly) completely mad; in that case, skip them and go on. However, it might be worth pausing before you do. I may be asking you to think from a point of view you don't usually assume; or you could vary the task yourself by approaching it from a new perspective. A writer's best gift is often the ability to question your own familiar assumptions, to look at something afresh.

(Writing drama is about being able to walk a mile in someone else's shoes: how else will you animate your characters in all their possible richness and variety?)

There isn't a right or wrong answer to any of the question exercises, so don't worry if your response differs from my comments; enjoy exploring and working towards an understanding of both. Record your responses in your writing diary, or on a computer, if you use one. That way, they will be available to you for future reference.

The book is arranged in seven chapters. Chapters 1 and 2 discuss relationships: between you, as playwright, and your audience; you and the production personnel; and between you, your story and the way you tell it. Chapters 3 to 6 collectively examine play structure. Each chapter takes one of four aspects, which I have termed 'fundamental dramatic principles': movement, action, conflict and juxtaposition. There are many different starting points from which to begin a play, and radically different styles of writing; I'm inviting you to look beneath the differences, and to see the same four principles interacting together, through character and story. The four principles are not arranged in order of priority, they are equal partners; but for ease of discussion, I've treated them in two pairs: movement and action, conflict and juxtaposition. Chapter 7 looks at writing the script itself, through dialogue and stage directions, beginning with practical suggestions about script layout and terminology.

Throughout, case studies offer a form of 'masterclass', where you can see playwrights using the ideas we're discussing, in fresh and individual ways. It's not essential for you to go and read each script in order to follow the case study, but I hope that you will read many of them afterwards. There are few better ways to develop your own craft than to read other writers' plays, and to see plays in performance.

But these must be balanced with as much writing practice as you can find time for; so theoretical discussion and case studies of other writers' plays always culminate in a piece of your own writing. At regular intervals throughout the book, there are checklists and summaries to be used as prompts when you're writing.

As an overall approach to your writing, you are encouraged to think in terms of formulating questions. It's a technique used variously by screenwriting experts (for example, Philip Parker in *The Art and Science of Screenwriting*), in actor and director training, and by many writers. I use them myself. But the technique is much older in origin; in Plato's *Dialogues*, the Greek philosopher Socrates is depicted using strategic questioning as a means of 'bringing thought to life... of making thought breathe' (as Franco Ruffini explains it, in *A Dictionary of Theatre Anthropology: the Secret Life of the Performer*.) For Socrates, this technique – maieutics – was itself an art, and like all art, is both a means of creating an understanding of the world around us, and also of communicating that understanding to others.

In this technique, formulation of the question itself matters much more than arriving at a definitive answer. American playwright Phyllis Nagy says, (*'Hold Your Nerve: Notes for a Young Playwright'*, in David Edgar's *State of Play*) 'there is never a single satisfactory answer to a complex question'. It is ultimately about cultivating an interrogative frame of mind, that is active, searching, flexible – and capable of being both surprised and delighted.

Surprise and delight are the points upon which this Introduction ends, and you will, I hope, begin. That's why my remarks on script layout are in Chapter 7 rather than Chapter 1. Though it's important to prepare the script properly before sending it to an agent or a theatre company, there is plenty of time to correct errors. Think, and write first, for the simple joy of experiment.

Write *for the pleasure*.

1 PLAYWRIGHT AND AUDIENCE

'You Talking To Me?'
(Travis Bickle in *Taxi Driver*, screenplay by Paul Schrader)

WHOSE PLAY IS IT, ANYWAY?

Many playwrights regard their plays as their 'children', and feel as emotionally involved with them and as fiercely protective as they would towards their actual children. I learned this the hard way when I was directing a new play by a first-time writer. He had written an intimate scene in which a boy and girlfriend lie in bed at three in the morning and confess to each other their deepest feelings and fears. It absolutely had to be performed in complete darkness, otherwise the couple wouldn't have had the nerve to admit those things. But it was close to eleven minutes long on the page – rather risky in performance without anything to look at; audiences tend to snooze when it's warm, dark and quiet! The scene needed editing down to around half its length to sharpen the emotional journey for both characters and thus to keep hold of the audience. As we sat down in the writer's kitchen to edit it (as dinner was cooking), he casually placed on the table between us, with the rest of the cutlery, an evil-looking bread knife. I thought, I do hope that's about bread. But it was also crystal clear to me, in that gesture (whether conscious or not), what was at stake for him. This play was his baby, and I was (literally) asking him to cut it.

The analogy with children is more than simply sentimental. As a child is composed from its parents' genetic material, so your play is composed from the many parts of you: your values and attitudes, the way you understand and respond to the world around you, your hopes, fears and desires, what you think and do in your daily life. Phyllis Nagy again: 'Plays are usually written by a single person in possession of an idiosyncratic style and point of view... intelligent, evocative and compelling.'

But you, the playwright, are not the sole parent; it is not only your 'material' which shapes your play in its fullest realization. The written script, that you will contribute, is one piece of what will eventually become a play. A *play* fully exists only when it is in performance before an audience, and thus it will accumulate 'material' contributed by actors, directors and designers, in the form of speech, gesture, movement, light, colour, textures, sound. Many of these may have been specified by you in the script, but some will not; they will be new, stimulated by what you have written. World theatre history shows us that there are only two constants in the creation of a play: the actor (who may or may not be human – think of puppets, or animals, for instance) and the audience. Does this mean therefore that the playwright is not essential, that when

Nagy speaks of 'the integrity of a single, abiding vision that yearns to communicate itself to willing audiences', she is merely 'talking up' the importance of the writer's role?

No, she isn't. Actor and audience both need and want a reason to come together, in that same place (the theatre, or performance arena) at the same time. It is you, the playwright, who answers their desire to create a shared experience; you answer it through your play, from your own 'yearning'. You don't originate the collective desire to share – we all have it, in many different forms – but you are most often the first to offer what is to be shared on this occasion: your 'idiosyncratic style and point of view' begins and shapes the process, giving it coherence, direction and force. We all come together because you have invited us.

The play, however, may not begin its life in scripted form; there are other ways in which plays are created, through improvisation and group devising in the rehearsal room with actors and perhaps also musicians and visual artists. But these are still understandable under the broad heading of 'playwriting', because someone begins the process and takes on the task of organizing and bringing together coherently all the various strands of 'material' contributed by members of the group. Though this person is not always described as a playwright (or scriptwriter), the process of organization, the creation of a coherent vision or argument to place before an audience, I also term writing.

CREATION AND INTERPRETATION

The last three paragraphs are not necessarily ones with which a lot of playwrights would concur. Many – indeed, most – insist on a separation between the *creation* of a play (your baby), by which is meant the writing of a playscript, and the *interpretation* of the script in production, by actor, director and designer. This division of roles, functions and responsibilities is concerned both with matters of ownership (reflected in copyright law – a means of protecting the baby, of giving it a surname), and also with controlling the many complex decisions which have to be taken in bringing a play to fruition with its audience. In this sense, the division between creation and interpretation is about status, respect and authority: whose say goes. In practice, however, in play production – particularly the play's first production – the division is rarely so clear-cut, and in the most successful production relationships, it should never be an issue. Some of the most celebrated elements of Tennessee Williams' classic play *A Streetcar Named Desire* were reportedly contributed by the director Elia Kazan, for example, and this is exactly how it should be: all parties completely in synch with the integrity of the play. It is an ideal relationship, but it is achievable, and it should be your goal.

The degree, and the nature, of the input from the production personnel continually shifts between the creative and the interpretative; this is acutely true where the script and the writer are taken through workshop prior to rehearsal, or as an integral part of the rehearsal process. Both workshop and rehearsal are actually a series of experiments and investigations, testing out the effectiveness of the play's component parts, altering what doesn't work, polishing and highlighting what does, whilst identifying the physical means of presentation to the audience.

THE PLAYWRIGHT'S PERSONAL STAKE

But 'ownership' is not simply a legal issue: it is also a very personal one for the playwright. Go back to our analogy with the child. Do parents 'own' their children? If you have children, would you describe your feelings towards them as 'proprietary'? The investment in them is certainly huge. There are rights, responsibilities and privileges in respect of them. They are, at every level, a part of one's self, one's life; they reflect back a profound sense of who and what one is. Other people are required to respect all of those things, and must not violate the boundaries between themselves and parent and child. And this is not a polite request; it is an imperative, and it will be fought for with – often – very great passion.

For many playwrights, these things are also true of their play, which is why you might feel the need to safeguard its integrity – its safety – with equal determination, perhaps even ferocity. But as a child has a life of its own, apart from its parent, so too does your play, as it grows from the script. Your investment, your rights and privileges, your sense of self: these are part of the process of writing, but they do not fully account for what a play is, and can be. For that, you have to think about the audience.

'A FORUM FOR DEBATE'

You write a play for your audience, because you have something you want to bring before their attention. It might be a particular topic, or a view about a topic. You want them to think about it, laugh, cry. Perhaps you want to challenge them to do something about it after they leave the theatre and re-enter their daily lives. The topic may be a burning one for you, and you would like the audience also to give it a high priority. (Think, for example, about the recent dramatization, in Britain, of the Stephen Lawrence murder case, or older plays such as Peter Weiss' *The Investigation*, about the Nuremberg Trials.) Timberlake Wertenbaker (writer of *Our Country's Good*) once said that, for her, theatre is a forum for debate; the play's task, therefore, is to generate the scope and the direction of the debate. It poses a question, makes a statement, shows a situation to the audience, and immediately we all pile in with our own ideas and responses. The script contains only part of the debate, its raw material; the debate proper begins once the audience sees and hears the script in performance and starts to talk back. It is the job of the script, and its performance, to provoke the audience into the debate.

In previous centuries, the debating process took a much more interactive form between play and audience, with members of the public contributing vocally or physically to the performance in progress. In some countries and forms of theatre, this is still the case today. In Britain however we tend to reserve that kind of active participation for Christmas pantomime or for stand-up comedy. In Western theatres we generally sit quietly in a darkened auditorium for short, intense periods of time, gazing at a pool of light that is physically separated from us. We show our responses subtly during the play, through giggles, sharp intakes of breath or sighs, or rustling when we've lost interest; only rarely do audiences utter actual words during a performance. Then we politely – sometimes enthusiastically – applaud the actors and go off to the bar, or straight home. If it has been a stimulating play, that is often where the debate happens most vociferously, where the play really begins to 'cook' – over a drink, or in the car, long after the actors, director and you, the playwright, have departed. But you are writing for that debate, to make it happen. Keep the barstool, the car, the living room in mind as you write, as well as the theatre; for that is where you want your audience to take your play – with them, wherever they go.

LIGHT RELIEF/DARK MATTER

Or perhaps what you want to bring to your audience isn't so pressing. Some playwrights say that they want simply to entertain, to allow the audience to step aside from their daily lives as a means of recreation. Plays are, after all, *play*. That doesn't necessarily mean that your play cannot be serious, or harrowing, or treat big subjects – entertainment is itself a process that is capable of running the gamut of emotional, intellectual and physical effects upon the audience. German playwright Bertolt Brecht, writing throughout the Nazi era, said that plays should be fun – fun to do, fun to watch, otherwise why bother? But he also described his ideal theatre as being like a boxing ring.

Think about those two things for a moment. Boxing would not be described, even by its aficionados, I imagine, as a light or trivial activity; it has many very dark aspects. But it is also exhilarating, challenging, riveting, both for those who find it barbaric as well as for those who love it. It is entertaining in the most complex, often polarizing sense: 'fun', in Brecht's meaning, which is to say 'energizing'. (And I say that as someone who doesn't like boxing.) Entertainment can, and I suggest should, exert this power to energize, provoke, divide or unite, whether or not you are setting out to wring your audience's withers, or amuse them with jokes about life's little idiosyncrasies. As playwright Peter Morris asserts, in response to fierce criticism of his play *The Age of Consent*, that tackles the subject of child murderers: 'Humour is not inconsistent with serious moral inquiry.'

As humans, we play as a means of remaking ourselves, of recharging our batteries. We also play as a means of exploring potential change and its consequences before we decide either to carry it out in our daily lives, or to abandon it. Play is a means by which we come to an understanding of ourselves and our place within the world. The particular forms our play takes are defining of us as humans; theatre is one of those forms. Your play, therefore, will fulfil a complicated and vital role; it will help to define you, the company that plays it, and the audience to whom and with whom it is played.

A SHARED EXPERIENCE

It is a big task, isn't it? That is why I have stressed that plays, in the fullest sense, are made by groups of people rather than solely by someone slaving away in isolation over a hot screen or wad of paper. The big task is shared throughout, and ultimately, this is why you write a play rather than a novel or a poem: you do it to get into the ring with other people, to be part of something, and to allow other people into the ring with you. It brings the writer who is relaxed and open enough to exploit this communal process fully the most exhilarating freedom. Of course you will accept some ideas and reject others offered by the other participants, but you are not – to use our analogy again – raising the baby alone. You have help. So, one of the most fundamental skills to learn, as a playwright, is how and when it is appropriate to give ground; to recognize help as help and not to reject it out of hand. We will try to explore here how to invite help through the ways in which the script is written. If you can do this, you will find that the playwright's role never ends, that you never, in fact, leave the process; for your invitations will continue to be taken up, by actor, director, designer and audience long after you have physically moved on.

FILLING THE EMPTY SPACE: THE AUDIENCE'S ROLE

'I can take any empty space and call it a bare stage. A man walks across this empty space

Why Write a Play?

What did you say in answer to this question? You might like to answer it again, before we progress. This time, in your response, be clear about what you want, what is at stake for you in writing a play – the one you already have at the back of your mind, I expect, if you have picked up this book. Phyllis Nagy called the impulse 'yearning'.

What is it for you?

If I were you, I would pin up that page over my desk while I wrote my play. It would keep me going, when I got stuck, or lost heart. It would keep me writing.

whilst someone else is watching him, and this is all that is needed for an act of theatre to be engaged.' (Peter Brook)

I have drawn a distinction between the script of a play that you may write in isolation, and the play itself that requires other people's input and the presence of an audience. This distinction would seem also to be true of film, television and radio dramas, too. Theatre plays, however, are rather different. They require the audience to be present within the same physical place and at the same time as the actors are performing the script and interacting with all the other elements of the production such as lighting, sound and set and costume design. Films, television and radio programmes nowadays are usually recorded; the actors are long gone by the time the audience comes to the play. A great deal of talk about the special nature and quality of theatre is vested in this simultaneous shared presence.

Theatre depends upon the shared presence because, during the processes both of writing a script and of rehearsing it, a particular role is created specifically for the audience to perform. That's why we don't tend to call rehearsal – or 'practice', as I have often heard

it termed in the United States – 'performance'; rehearsal is strategic planning and exploration that tries out lots of possibilities for bringing the script to the audience and the audience into the play. We spend our time in rehearsal creating the means by which the debate with the audience can be brought to occur; that is, we collectively 'write in' the audience's role, but we have to wait until opening night for them to perform it for the first time. When they do, they do it simultaneously with our performing of the script, and thus both their performance and ours continually adjusts, moment by moment. This dynamic and instantaneous reciprocal transaction is unique and fundamental to theatre. It is only at this point that the theatre play is fully alive, and it is this element that gives theatre its most complex, and often disturbing, quality .

In theatre, this requirement to write in the audience's role begins with you as playwright, and it means we also have to think about the context or situation in which the performance takes place, and about creating a receptive mood. So we should consider where and how the audience and the play will come together physically, in order to encourage them also to come together intellectually and emotionally. We have to think about the stage and its relationship to the space that the audience occupies – and about why this relationship matters. Obviously you hope that your (successful) play will be performed in lots of different theatres, so this would seem to be quite a complicated matter, as you are writing your play, not directing or producing it.

EXERCISE

- Think about someone you know who is wonderful at telling jokes. (Maybe you're good at it yourself.)
- Now think about someone who is really terrible at this.

- What is the difference between them? (Assume that they are both telling the same joke, so the difference doesn't lie in the words of the joke.) Why does one person make you laugh while the other doesn't?
- Even better, think of someone who is so good at this that s/he can make you laugh at something that isn't even funny.
- How is this achieved?

Comments

You may have thought of a number of answers, such as:

- Timing
- Use of pauses
- Facial expressions or accompanying gestures
- Emphasis of certain key words
- Tone of voice
- The situation or context you're in when the joke is being told
- The mood you're in – whether or not you are predisposed to laugh, or whether you're feeling cranky, or miserable.

The first five are performance techniques, and they will vary from joke to joke, from teller to teller. But the one element all good joke tellers share is that they understand precisely how they need you, their audience, to respond to each moment of the joke, what they need you actually to do. And thus they select their technical means of performing the joke (such as the five listed above) so as to get you to do what they need – when to wait, when to anticipate, when to be caught on the hop, and how to react to each of those things.

STAGE AND AUDITORIUM

I'm going to assume that, if you have chosen to write a stage play, you've probably seen at least one play in a theatre before, or perhaps been in a play. What was the theatre like? Large or small? Was it a place built as a theatre, or was it a space designed for some other function but now permanently adapted for theatre, as quite a number of former churches or warehouses have been? Or was it 'borrowed' temporarily for a production (such as a church hall, or somebody's garden?) Was it in the street? (There are, for example, companies who perform short scenes on underground trains, and others who will, for a small sum, come and perform in your living room.)

Think back: what was the spatial relationship between the stage (where the actors were) and the audience's area? How did that arrangement help (or hinder) your engagement with the play?

EXERCISE

In Figures 1–4 (pages 18–20):

- Where do you think the actors and scenery (if there is any) would most likely be?
- Where would the audience most likely be?
- Are the actors and the audience kept separate, or are they intermingled?
- What kind of adjectives would you choose to describe the relationship between the actors' space and the audience's space? (For example, close, intimate, claustrophobic, warm, involved/distant, cool/cold, isolated, and so on.)
- Do you think that, in each of the illustrations, the audience would feel involved or immersed in the play, or do you think they would feel as if they were 'outside looking in', perhaps even 'spying on' or 'peeping at' what is going on onstage?

COMMENTS

Your immediate response to my questions may well have been: 'it depends on the play'. Of

Figure 1   In the round.

Figure 2   Amphitheatre.

Figure 3   Courtyard.

Figure 4   Studio Theatre.

course this is true, since these are all spaces that could accommodate, at different times, lots of different plays. But it's also true that certain kinds of theatre spaces serve some plays better than others. Cameron Mackintosh, one of the most successful contemporary British theatre producers, says that he goes to great lengths to 'cast the theatre' for his latest production, in the same way that the director casts a play with the most appropriate actors. And in many post-1960 theatres, built as studios (*see* Fig. 4), one of the key architectural features is the ability to change completely the internal layout of the stage and auditorium spaces through flexible seating arrangements. This is precisely so that the special needs of each different play might be answered, literally by bringing actors and audience into varying kinds of proximity.

Over and above the exact nature and form of the play being performed at any given time, there are certain kinds of relationships implied by theatre architecture. Of course, the playwright doesn't have to worry about the specific architecture of a theatre space, that is someone else's task. But you do have to think, right from the beginning of working on your script, about the special qualities of the relationship you want to create between the actors – who will, by that point, have embodied your characters – and your audience; that is, you have to think about the relationship that is at the heart of your play. From this will come your stagecraft.

DISTANCE, PROXIMITY AND FEELING: CREATING 'AFFECTIVE SPACE'

What kind of adjectives did you choose, in the exercise, to describe the nature of that relationship, and the audience's responses? Those adjectives are the ones for which you, as playwright, need to write. You need to know the kinds of feelings and thoughts you want your audience to have whilst watching the play – perhaps even to the point of knowing that you want them to experience physical sensations. For these are absolutely fundamental to the role you write for your audience to play. And of course you will want them to carry those thoughts and feelings, the memory of those physical sensations, with them when they leave the theatre and continue their dialogue of debate with the play.

Irrespective of the particular architecture of the theatre in which a play is actually performed, the relationship between audience and play has to be created first within the script itself: completely embedded in the characters and the structure of the story. The production follows the writer's lead. The nature of the relationship is determined by you, as playwright, right from the beginning of the scriptwriting process; one of the main tasks in rewriting is to deepen and clarify it.

Once you have a sense of how you need the audience to engage, try to express it in your writing diary in terms of *distance*. Do you, for instance, want them to feel as if they're 'in it', as if it is happening to them right there and then? Do you want it to feel very real? Then you need them, in terms of distance, to be 'very close'. Does that mean they have therefore to be sitting physically close to the actors? It might do; so you may find that what you are writing is a small-scale chamber play, for a little theatre, rather than something on an epic scale, appropriate to the vast stage of a big lyric theatre or arena.

However, this need not exclude such largeness of physical scale. You can bring us

The Woman in Black

In Stephen Mallatratt's adaptation of Susan Hill's ghost story, it's essential that the audience is as unnerved by the strangeness of the unfolding events as is the young man to whom they are actually happening in the story. And so the habitual conditions of a darkened, largely silent auditorium, with our attention focused on the lit areas of the stage, which show us some things but not others – a state of affairs over which the audience has no control – lend themselves to this essential requirement. It's of little consequence whether or not members of the audience know exactly how the particular relationship between them and the experience of the story is being created; it still achieves its effect. When I saw the play several years ago, I knew perfectly well how each element of the play was put together, how each special effect was done, but it made not a jot of difference to my reactions whilst watching. I still squeaked and shivered along with everyone else, and was still sufficiently queasy to keep a night-light on in my house for a few days afterwards! Despite my technical knowledge, the play still 'got to me'. It worked because I was made to feel that I was immersed in the same situation as the central character at the same time; vulnerable and at risk, just as he was.

Copenhagen

The audience may need to remain cool and detached emotionally from the action, but thoroughly involved intellectually, as is the case in Michael Frayn's *Copenhagen*, a play about Niels Bohr and Werner Heisenberg, quantum physics, the Uncertainty Principle and the atom bomb. In its première production, this relationship was physically created by the audience surrounding the action, as if perhaps they were themselves scientists in a laboratory, minutely studying an experiment. The stage was fully illuminated, nothing was concealed, and it was possible also to see the other audience members. This encompassing spatial relationship and visibility was maintained even when the production transferred to a different theatre with an entirely different architectural layout. This suggests that the spatial relationship between audience and play was not a directorial or designer's whim, but was absolutely fundamental to the experience of the play: it had been created by Michael Frayn, and physicalized by the production team. Yet Frayn, in the published text, gives not even one stage direction as to the physical layout of the play; he doesn't need to, for the relationship is embedded within the script structure, within the way the story is told.

very close in other ways; through character, for example. Shakespeare's *Hamlet* is, in every respect, a large play, yet it is also a play that brings its audience into very close proximity. It's done through the central character of Hamlet himself. Though he is remote from us in terms of social status – he is a Prince – and his story is quite melodramatic (murder, ghosts, madness and suicide, not exactly most audiences' everyday experience), the journey he travels is one many of us are likely to know personally. He is a young man struggling to come to terms with the death of his idolized father, and feeling very acutely the emotional pain of loss and also of disappointment in the apparent lack of sympathy and parallel distress exhibited by those closest to him. This enveloping and disorientating anguish is a familiar, recurring human experience.

That's the starting point of Hamlet's journey, and it is the fact that we can immediately recognize what it is he feels that draws us close to him. The unfolding of the story will take Hamlet into a nightmarish series of events that threaten his sanity and his life, and he will have to work out, on the hoof, what to do about them. By the end of the play, one way or another, he will have done it. The specific details of the story are rather fantastical; we are kept close by what is familiar – the emotional roller-coaster he rides, the worry and periods of indecision about what to do and whether it is right or not. And he talks to us continually throughout the play, giving us access to his most private thoughts and feelings. Though *Hamlet* is a large play, in terms of distance, it's a very intimate one.

In choosing adjectives to describe the relationship implied by the physical conditions in the exercise photographs, you 'characterized' the relationship. Now add to your expression the distance or proximity of the relationship you want your audience to have with your play, a sense of how you want it to *feel*. In *The Woman in Black*, for example, the closeness felt, to me, claustrophobic, like a trap. It is a 'haunted house' story, but this is actually a physical metaphor for every enclosed, concealing space in which you have ever felt yourself to be ill at ease. It is a metaphoric vessel for your deepest fears. It doesn't matter whether what you fear really is ghosts, or darkness: these are themselves metaphors for the fear of danger, for fear itself.

In *Copenhagen*, where detachment – a degree of distance – is required, I suggested 'cool' as an adjective. 'Clinical' might also be appropriate. But 'cold' would not be right, for what is at stake in the play is too urgent for that. Two great scientists are wrangling with the morality of translating their intellectual expertise into the reality of military technology; morality, expediency, control, self-preservation are all in play. These themes might be thought of as 'white-hot', and could draw us in very close; instead, Frayn holds us at arm's length by creating a series of intellectual hypotheses. We watch the two scientists wrestling with these imperatives exactly as they wrestle with their science: hypothesis, argument, evidence, proof, new hypothesis. But just as they also feel the passion of their cerebral enquiries and discoveries, so too they are not immune to the emotions of the moral imperatives. And neither are we, as we work through the same intellectual process with them. So, while there is coolness here, there is not coldness. It is a laboratory, not an icebox.

You will notice that I am using both the reality of physical space and the way it makes us feel – *affective space* – to help you clarify the mental and emotional relationships between your play and your audience. Just as the process of 'writing out' in your diary helps to prime the transfer of your thoughts into a physical form, thinking about affective space can crystallize for you one of the fundamental aspects of your play.

WHO ARE YOU TALKING TO?

In order to know what kind of relationship you want to generate, you must think specifically about whom you are addressing, for 'the audience' is not an abstract entity; it is a group of people, each of them distinct, with different kinds of knowledge and experience. So you must identify what will bind them, for the duration of your play, into a collective entity that is able to share the experience and engage mutually in the debate. You need to know what your play is really 'about' – and by this, I don't simply mean the story, or its themes (though you will need to understand those); I mean that you need to know what is the true nature of the communication you wish to provoke between you all. Once you have a grasp of this – and it may not be wholly clear to you at the outset of writing, but should become so as you progress – you will find it also becomes clear how that communication is to be constructed and understood. That is, you will see where and how you need to call into play the audience's imagination.

Imagination is at the heart of our human capacity to create stories, which we both want and need to do; it's a means of answering both

'On Your Imaginary Forces Work'

(Shakespeare, *Henry V*)
Imagination is the most crucial component of theatre. It is both a faculty – the means by which the play is fully created, by you (the writer), the production personnel, and the audience – and a creative act itself, something which is carried out by all parties involved. But what actually is it? Dictionaries define imagination as the formation of a mental image of something that is not actually present in reality, synonymous with fancy, fantasy, falsehood, delirium, ecstasy, dream, nightmare, mirage, hallucination (amongst others). It is, in other words, our innate human ability to make something out of next to nothing, to build an elaborate mental construction from a very little stimulus.

our desires and our necessities. But nothing comes from nothing, and imagination doesn't function without a stimulus to trigger it. This is where, as a technique, asking questions is helpful. Asking questions encourages us to formulate propositions or hypotheses – potential answers – and to do so, we use our imaginative faculty to make links between what we know and what we guess. Making those links is the core of the imaginative act; it is a wholly creative act, which is original and particular to each person involved – to you, to the actor, to the audience member. It will be slightly different in each person's case, because each person's knowledge and experience is unique.

If each person's imagination will produce different links, different potential answers to the propositions raised by your questions, how are you to create any kind of collective understanding? Let's take an example, to see how the shared experience can work.

THE SERVANT (LYRIC THEATRE, HAMMERSMITH, 2001)

In Neil Bartlett's reworking of Robin Maugham's 1958 play *The Servant* at the Lyric Theatre Hammersmith – based by Maugham on his own 1948 novella – a post-play discussion between Bartlett, the actors and the audience produced a striking range of commonality. The play follows the fortunes of a rich young man, Tony, who hires a servant, Barrett, to run his house in Chelsea. In the course of the play, their roles are spectacularly reversed, and Barrett gains complete ascendancy over his 'master' by orchestrating the gratification of all of Tony's desires, spoken and unspoken. After the performance, two key questions were asked by the audience: 'Why does Barrett do it?' and 'What happens next to the characters?' (that is, after the story ends).

'Why does Barrett do it?' brought immediate smiles from the cast and director; of course, this would have been an intriguing question for them in rehearsal. It's a question which is never answered, either within the play or Maugham's novella. Actor Michael Feast, who played Barrett, teased us by admitting that he had his own ideas about Barrett's reasons, but wasn't going to tell us what they were. Then he laughed and said, actually, he'd be quite happy to tell *us*, but not for *them* to know (his fellow actors). And though this was playful on Feast's part, it was also absolutely correct: 'Why does Barrett do it?' is the question that animates the entire play. The propositions built by the rest of the cast, and by each of us, in attempting to answer that question, are not only what the play is about (the core of the communication); they are also how the play works (how the communication is constructed and understood). There isn't a single (or simple) answer to this question; it is maieutic – the whole point is the company's and our continuing to chew upon it, for then we delve deeper into the heart of the play.

Neil Bartlett later told me that a frequent post-play response from audience members was to say that they 'felt like going home and taking a shower', and he was quite satisfied with that. The propositions we create in attempting to answer core questions are not always safely contained within the cerebral level as mental hypotheses; they frequently seep into the realms of feeling and physical sensation. Those audience members who felt like taking a shower were expressing, very vividly, a strong physical sense of having been 'smeared' by the propositions thrown up by the play, and you can hear, in their response, the power of imagination at work. Phyllis Nagy says 'If we are able to definitively answer questions about why our plays exist or what they mean, then our plays do not allow for active communication with an audience.' By 'definitively' Nagy means not creating or predetermining a single answer (which runs the risk of closing down the imagination); rather, it means opening up the possibility of multiple answers, allowing the imagination free rein. Some of those possible answers will be thought, some will be felt; many will move between mind, body and emotions. Powering them all is the imagination.

Neil Bartlett pointed out that neither the script nor the production of *The Servant* predetermines for us how we are to understand or evaluate Barrett's actions (or indeed, anything else in the play). We are compelled to construct our own reading, within our own moral framework. We are compelled because we watch Barrett performing a series of escalating actions that irrevocably turn the tables on Tony, and we can't believe Tony doesn't see it. So a second, perhaps even more engrossing question is thrown up by our attempts to answer 'Why does Barrett do it?'; that is, 'Why doesn't Tony stop it?'

The audience's second question, 'What happens next to the characters?' provoked an intriguing response from actor Jack Davenport, who played Tony; intriguing, because he actually offered (from his point of view) an answer to the other question 'Why doesn't Tony stop it?' instead. Davenport's answer was that Tony 'may be on the edge of a precipice, but he quite likes what he sees at the bottom'. In other words, Tony doesn't stop what is happening because he is enjoying both the risk and the return; and therefore, 'What happens next?', in Tony's case, is that he's going to keep right on accepting Barrett's offers, whatever the eventual consequences. Then Davenport acknowledged that this would not be the audience's expected answer: 'Now, after that bombshell...' And he was quite right; it wasn't my answer, for instance, up to that point. But now, because of his answer, mine is shifting in response: a whole new raft of questions is

provoked, and some of those questions are more about me and the way I see the world than they are about Barrett and Tony. Davenport's answer was not definitive, in the sense of being the only one possible; it was not even the one with which he began, in rehearsal. His own initial answer was challenged and modified by Neil Bartlett's.

QUESTIONS AND ANSWERS

The beauty of maieutic questions is their ability immediately to generate more questions the moment we arrive at a possible answer. Maieutic questioning is thus an ongoing process, and this is how the debate is provoked. So the differences between our various attempts to answer core questions aren't a recipe for confusion, after all: they are actually the debate itself in full swing.

What is shared by both company and audience is an agreement as to the nature of the questions that drive the play, and the ways in which we construct hypothetical answers to them – what we draw upon in order to answer. We draw upon our collective understanding of human behaviour (particularly transgressive behaviour), our shared moral frame of reference, our grasp of social hierarchies. But in our attempts to call upon them, we find a sharp and sometimes shocking divergence of opinion. We find that while we may agree on the questions, we don't automatically share even the components of the possible answer, let alone the answer itself. This calls into (new) question our assumptions about our understanding of human behaviour, our moral frame of reference, and social hierarchies.

This is how you harness the imagination in writing: by allowing the divergence of opinion to work for rather than against you. Actively solicit it by constructing core questions to drive the play, questions that everyone has to ask –

25

director, actor, audience. And predict at least some of the ways in which they will all try to construct their proposed answers; understand what they will draw upon in terms of their real-life knowledge. Constructing core questions and projecting possible ways of answering them forms the central work of structuring your play. Questions help you discover what your play is really about – what the true nature of your communication is, and will then help you 'open negotiations with the audience', as it were.

For some writers, formulating core questions can be preliminary work, applied to the idea for a play when it first occurs, as a means of turning the idea into a story. If you can use questions right from the outset, they can save you a lot of time, because they point to the shape and focus of your story. But don't worry if this isn't the most productive way of working for you. For other writers, core questions only start to become clear after they have written a rough draft of the script and are beginning to rewrite. One writer described this way of working as 'getting out of the way of the story that is trying to tell me what it is'. What he meant by that is the subject of Chapter 2.

2 PLAYWRIGHT AND STORY: THE IDEA OF THE PLAY

A PERSONAL 'VOICE'

Writers are frequently asked where they get their ideas from, as if there is a kind of bran tub of wizard wheezes into which you can plunge your hand and come up with an award-winner. There isn't, of course. The simple answer is that the idea for the play comes from within you. Earlier, I suggested that your play will be composed from 'your values and attitudes, the way you understand and respond to the world around you, your hopes, fears and desires, what you think and do in your daily life'. These are the wellsprings of your ideas, and the source of your own distinctive writer's 'voice'. But this doesn't automatically mean that you will be writing an autobiography (although you might choose to do that).

It does mean, however, that many aspects of you will be embedded within your play, and it is awareness of this deeply personal involvement that is the source of much of the tension and insecurity writers can feel (as well as intense exhilaration) when their script goes into workshop or rehearsal. Many of the heated arguments that can occur there are not as often as they might appear, solely about defending the dramatic integrity of a particular script detail. They are also about protecting the degree of self-exposure – the writer's high personal stakes – that the script detail makes inevitable. In your play, you will (I hope you will) give yourself away – be willing to put the opinions, ideas, passions and prejudices that shape you into the 'forum for debate' of which Timberlake Wertenbaker spoke. For if you are brave enough to put yourself on the line first by writing your own vulnerability into your script, then your courage calls into action that of the production personnel – most especially, the actors – and that of the audience. This is, I believe, as true of comedy as it is of the most serious drama; perhaps even more so, since in choosing the medium of comedy you will be exposing those 'embedded' aspects to the challenge of laughter.

'Dirty laundry' (as Abi Morgan puts it) is what writers have to find the courage to show to audiences: the aspects of human beliefs and behaviour, social mores and moralities, that show us at our most complex and provocative – our dark as well as our light side. If you, as playwright, can do this, we will respond – sometimes with anger and argument, sometimes with laughter and pleasure, but always, I think, with relief that someone has thought us worthy of the challenge. Then theatre really is worth its salt.

But it's rarely your literal 'dirty laundry' you are going to put before us. In Chapter 1, I suggested you might think about the relationship between your play and your audience in terms of distance. If it is the case that you, as writer, are very deeply embedded in your play, then the 'affective space' is also between your audience and you yourself. And so it is clear that the issue of distance or

Writers and their plays

Listen to Martin McDonagh on *The Lieutenant of Inishmore* that treats Irish nationalism and violence through black comedy: 'I thought I should tackle the problems on my own side. I'm not being heroic or anything – it was just something I felt I had to write about. The play came from a position of what you might call pacifist rage.' Asked by interviewer Sean O'Hagan if he thought that perhaps comedy was an inappropriate medium, his reply was unequivocal: 'No... I walk that line between comedy and cruelty because I think one illuminates the other. And I tend to push things as far as I can because I think you can see things more clearly through exaggeration than through reality.' (*The Guardian*, 24 March 2001). *The Lieutenant of Inishmore* provoked heated debate, much of it challenging McDonagh's taste, judgement and personal values in colliding that subject matter with this dramatic form. But for a writer of passion such as McDonagh is, 'I don't feel I have to defend anything, really.' 'Surely,' he says, 'we should be writing stuff that stirs it up.'

Or to Mark Ravenhill, talking to Kate Kellaway (*The Observer Review*, 19 August 2001) about *Mother Clap's Molly House*: 'It is so personal. It is about my obsessions and fantasies and fears.' And to Abi Morgan (*The Guardian*, 25 July 2001): '*Tender* is my most strongly autobiographical play. It is about how difficult it is to hold on to relationships. There is a line in the play: 'It's not that I believe everyone will leave, but I can't contemplate the idea they will stay.' Journalist Lyn Gardner asked her if this was how she herself felt. 'Not any more. I've moved on in the year since I wrote that.' For years, Abi Morgan didn't show her plays to anyone, until she found a director who could 'make you a braver writer than you feel you are. I wouldn't mind showing my dirty laundry to her.'

proximity is of vital importance: how close do you want, or need, the audience to be to you?

I went on to say, in Chapter 1, that activating the audience's imagination is central to the process of promoting the desired communication between you both, within this affective domain. Imagination is also the key to the construction of distance between the literal details of your own life, thoughts, values, and the specifics of your play: its story, its world, its characters. If you quake at the prospect of such self-exposure, imagination offers you a means of shielding the extent of your vulnerability, by transforming it through dramatic metaphor. Finding the appropriate metaphor in a potential idea is, therefore, an important task.

LOCATING METAPHOR: WRITE WHAT YOU UNDERSTAND

Novice writers in search of ideas are frequently told to 'write what you know'. This can often seem very dismal advice. If you haven't led a life of enormous variety (yet), you may well feel that your daily routines are not what you want to write about. It can be quite dull enough living them; what you really want to do, through your writing, is something else, to go somewhere else, be someone else. Phyllis Nagy, once again, helps us: 'Plays are not journalism.' She is very firm on this point: 'The literal workings of the world and its minutiae have never been, and must never become, anything other than the tools we use to construct lateral work, which communicates metaphor.'

Well, it is true that some plays are journalism – I referred earlier to dramatizations of the Stephen Lawrence case and the Nuremberg Trials, for example, that depend for their content upon transcripts of actual judicial proceedings. But those plays are not only journalism; they share with other good plays the ability to transcend reportage – the simple recording of events and words – through the construction and activation of metaphor. Metaphor bridges the journalistic and the imaginative: it describes one thing in terms usually applied to something else, and in doing so, implies a comparison between them. For example, we speak of 'the scales of justice', a metaphor of weights and measures which implies that the judicial process is one of balance and equality. Metaphor is therefore able to compare ideas and concepts as well as material aspects.

To help you begin to think more freely in terms of dramatic metaphor, instead of 'write what you know' (which we tend to interpret as 'know because we live it on a daily basis'), substitute 'understand': 'write what you understand.' Something quite different happens; the journalistic recording of daily experience loses something of its restrictive curb on the imagination.

THE PRISONER'S DILEMMA (2001)

David Edgar's play The Prisoner's Dilemma can help us explore the imaginative connections between 'understanding' and dramatic metaphor.

Edgar set out to write the third in a trilogy of plays set in Europe after the end of the Cold War. The play's subject is peace processes, the often protracted series of negotiations that, in seeking to end wars, seem to replicate them in a different arena. In his research for the play, Edgar found a game model known as 'Prisoner's Dilemma', in which two (hypothetical) criminals are arrested and separately offered the chance to escape charges if they will incriminate the other. (You may recognize this ploy, so far: it's a very familiar scenario in TV police dramas!) The twist, however, is that if both prisoners incriminate each other, then the punishment for each will be harsher than if they had both said nothing. The choices are starkly clear:

- If A (as Edgar puts it) 'rats out' B, A goes free and B goes to prison, or vice versa (B rats out A).
- If A rats out B and B rats out A, both go to prison for much longer.
- If neither says anything, the sentence will be shorter, but both will go to prison.

The central problem is one of trust: as Edgar says, 'If you do what's best for you (whatever the other guy decides) your best option is to rat. However, if you do what's best for the other guy – miraculously – you both end up better off. The risk is that you have to rely on the other guy being smart enough or nice enough to work that out.' The tension here between self-interest and altruism is something each of us can understand perfectly well. I doubt that many of us have had to make a choice where what is at stake is as acute as it is for the prisoners – that is, we are unlikely to have lived this scenario – but we have all wrestled at many points of our lives with problems of trust. In the end, we understand, whatever the specifics of the occasion, it always comes down to the same point: someone has to make the leap of faith, and make it first.

So, we understand Prisoner's Dilemma: it is a neat and clear metaphor. It invites us to make comparisons between A and B and ourselves, and by setting up an opposition between A's and B's points of view, it dramatizes our comparison. We have to shift between the various choices within the scenario. We have to go beyond the simple hypothesis of 'if A rats out B,' and ask a much more personal question: 'if I were A (or B), which option would I choose?' To try to answer that, you have to ask 'am I willing or able to be the one to make the leap of faith?' Whichever you answer, yes or no, you will have acknowledged an even deeper question about the ways in which your own relationships of trust (or lack of) are constructed, and lived. This is because there won't be a single definitive answer; it is likely that you will have run through, in your head, a wealth of situations and contexts, in some of which you would have been willing and able, and some of which you wouldn't.

Emotional understanding

'Understand' prompts you to find the emotional threads running through stories, for they are familiar and recurring. Once you recognize that the same emotional undercurrents may be present in two quite different situations, you are led to think about what else may also be alike. And it may be that in this dialogue between thinking and feeling, you can find the dramatic metaphor that will drive a play.

Why not, instead, substitute 'feel' for 'know': 'write what you feel'? 'Feel' is a driving force behind television soap operas, and evokes powerful reciprocal emotions in the audience. But whilst the stories make emotional sense, they don't always give the brain anything equally stimulating to do. 'Understand' reminds you to speak to both head and heart; for the leap between emotion and intellect is the leap of imagination and intuition.

A GOOD IDEA? – THE PROMISE OF ENERGY AND MOVEMENT

The metaphor of Prisoner's Dilemma is not inert, it's dynamic; it keeps on generating different positions and hypotheses – new 'ifs'. And while it provokes you into revealing truths about yourself as you explore the various questions it raises, the metaphor also provides the degree of distance that protects you: after all, A and B are not you, and Prisoner's Dilemma is not something you have literally lived. It is a game hypothesis. Distance here is crucial, and also paradoxical. Because you have the safety of the metaphor as a shield, you are able to reveal much more, to allow the audience much closer to you. The metaphor allows you to invoke contrast (difference) as well as comparison (likeness), and it is from the dynamism of this juxtaposition that drama draws its power.

This metaphor is inherently dramatic because it is constantly in action, and keeps us constantly in motion in trying to explore it: intellectually and emotionally we shift position repeatedly within the affective space of the relationship between audience and play. When you are considering an idea for a play, look for this inherent capacity for movement, in the form of 'energy'.

When we watch people or things moving in everyday life, the signs of energy are often what strike us: the speed of a car, or the buoyancy of someone's walk. In speech, we hear the gush of energy in a person who talks a mile a minute. These are instances of energy discharged or expressed. It's usual when a quantity of energy is expressed in this way that a great deal of movement occurs, and it's quite exciting to observe.

But we observe a different quality when energy is held back or compressed. Often, in such situations, movement or speech is artificially slower, buoyancy suppressed. Think of the small child ordered to 'walk, don't run', who obeys but is still dying to dash off. Or of the person in an argument who is trying to get a word in edgewise amid the other one's torrent. In such cases, the energy can't find an outlet for full expression, and so remains latent – until it finds its moment, spies its opening and bang! The force of the discharge is all the greater for the energy having been previously held back. The greater the compression imposed by resistance, the more intensely dramatic the eventual expression will be, and the sharpness of contrast between repression and expression is even more exciting to observe.

When you are considering an idea, it is this quality of latent, or compressed, energy you should try to locate in it. The difficult task for writers really isn't having an idea in the first place – you will probably have lots of those. The difficult task is developing a story out of the initial idea, because only once you begin to do that will you discover whether or not your idea can yield a dynamic dramatic metaphor. Developing an idea into a story means finding a way in which the energy that is latent in the idea can express itself, through metaphor, with sufficient force and focus to engage an audience. Such expression will require time and space in which to occur, the time and space of a play. Think in terms of movement – movement in time and through time, in space and through space. An idea has to have somewhere to go; if it hasn't, it is a conceit rather than a dramatic idea, and it won't drive a play.

EXERCISE
- In the case of David Edgar's play, would you say the 'idea' was that he wanted to write about peace processes? Given Edgar's declared interest in exploring contemporary political subjects, this certainly offers a starting point. But is it a dramatic idea in itself?
- If you think it is, try to describe what you think is the latent energy in that idea. What is exciting about it? What kind of story does it suggest to you? What kinds of questions does it bring to your mind?

COMMENTS
In his *Guardian* article (7 July 2001) about the writing of the play (from which my earlier quotations are also taken), Edgar comments that, in the case of peace processes, 'it was obvious that such rich interpersonal drama lent itself to dramatisation'. He notes, a few lines further on, that 'as well as being a suitable medium for dealing with peace processes, drama is also a metaphor and a means for the process itself'. There is a clear forward step here, from finding the topic of

A dramatic conceit

There's a neat example that came up in a recent writing workshop. Paul, whose special talent is for writing comedies with wildly surreal moments, was pitching ideas to the workshop leader. 'There's this ballerina in a mental institution who can see Skippy the Kangaroo there. We think she's hallucinating the kangaroo, but it's really Skippy who's hallucinating the ballerina!' The workshop leader laughed. 'That's very funny. And then...?' Silence. 'What happens next?' 'Errr...' That's a conceit: if no 'and then...' springs to mind, you probably don't have the makings of a dramatic story. 'And then...?' is rather a handy little acid test of a first idea. But Skippy and the ballerina is a nice gag! (My thanks to Paul for permission to use it here.)

peace processes suitable for dramatization, to identifying that the process of drama itself is a very precise metaphor for the process of peace negotiation.

It seems that Edgar found the metaphor when he discovered that international peace negotiators are increasingly being trained by means of role-play games (such as Prisoner's Dilemma), and that, indeed, much of the contemporary theory of peacemaking is governed by 'game theory'. This is where the dramatic idea is truly located, because it is full of latent energy: it just teems with questions and possibilities. Who trains them? Where? In what kind of situation or environment? What kind of role-play scenarios do they use? How do they know if they're right? What would 'right' be? What happens when they do it for real? Does the hypothetical training work? If peacemaking is based on game theory, is warmaking based on that, too? (A very disturbing element about the Cuban Bay of Pigs crisis in 1962 was the link between the American/Russian stand-off over siting of nuclear weapons and the involvement of game theorists advising the Pentagon.) What happens if, in the real situation, the participants don't 'play the game'? *Is this really a game?*

These (or similar) are probably the kinds of questions that occurred to David Edgar. You can hear in them the beginnings of the conversion from idea to story – the ways in which the latent energy in the idea might express itself through a play. People, situations and actions begin to propose themselves: there are hints about the ways in which time and space might be organized, and movement articulated. The big arc of movement is likely to be the crossover between the hypothetical role-play situation and the real peace negotiations, and thus the dramatic shape is going to emerge from the comparison and contrast between the two. Other kinds of

movement will occur, as people's positions are changed (political, intellectual, emotional). This is indeed how Edgar eventually structured the play. Act One Scene One explores the role-play training within a university environment; subsequent scenes move between the real theatre of war and the negotiating table proper, as the theory is attempted in practice.

So in answer to my question, I would say that wanting to write about peace processes was not itself the dramatic idea. That desire sent Edgar in search of the idea. The dramatic idea arose from the discovery of the metaphor. That's where questions can really ignite the writer's imagination. The process of questioning releases the latent energy in the idea, and the transformation from dramatic idea into dramatic story is under way.

Ask the Right Question

Many new writers have a strong sense of what they want to write about; I'm often told, these days, 'I have an idea for a play about child abuse.' (It's a socially important subject, and one which arouses powerful emotions.) I say 'Tell me the idea.' And we hit a wall, because although they may have a topic, they don't necessarily yet have a dramatic idea, and thus can't proceed. So I ask 'What are the questions buzzing around in your mind about this?' One writer might say 'What kind of person does that? Why would they do it?'; another, 'What kind of damage does it do?'; another, 'How do you keep children safe? Who can you trust?' Then we're in business; the questions spark the beginnings of the idea and the inklings of a story.

STORIES AND STORYTELLING

There's a great deal of discussion in the professional drama industries about just how many types of dramatic story there actually are. Student writers are often appalled by the notion that there are 'story types' at all, since this appears to cast doubt on their originality. But we've all experienced, in watching a bad play or film, the dismal sense of déjà vu when we recognize the story and consequently know exactly what's going to happen next, and how and when. In a really poor piece, it's even possible to 'sing along' with the dialogue as it happens, so predictable is it all. So we tend to lose interest in watching any further.

But in watching a good play or film, the same thing usually happens: we recognize the story. But we don't lose interest. Instead, we're delighted by the recognition. We start to play, guessing what will happen next, and how it will happen. We enjoy it when we guess right, and enjoy it when we guess wrong and something else happens instead. So why is it that recognition and prediction are absorbing in one case, but not in the other?

One major difference lies in what is genuinely original, and that's you and your audience. The story may be familiar but you haven't told this story before; or if you have, elsewhere, you haven't told it to this audience before. Even if they've heard it before, they've not heard it from you. So what makes a substantial difference is precisely the element we considered earlier: the extent to which you are present – embedded – within the play, and the relationship you set up between you, your play and your audience. Plays that don't hold our interest are usually ones where the writer seems to be absent or untraceable. We often describe such plays as having no 'writer's voice'. Plays that do hold us are ones where we can find you, where we can hear your distinctive voice talking to us.

There is a vital relationship to be explored, therefore, between the familiar story type and your particular way of telling it. Shakespeare's *Romeo and Juliet* and Jonathan Harvey's *Beautiful Thing*, for example, are both romances, in terms of story type, but Jonathan Harvey tells his story quite differently from the way Shakespeare tells his: Harvey's romantic couple are both male, for example. And whereas Shakespeare's couple are finally united in death, Harvey's are still alive and kicking at the end of the play. The one is a tragedy, the other isn't.

Differences of storytelling – in genre, character and outcome, in this example – create wholly different relationships with their respective audiences. And in so doing, they produce, from a common story type, individual stories that are freshly-minted.

Consider these two statements:

- the story that you're telling is dependent on the way you tell the story
- the way you tell the story is dependent on the story that you're telling

They seem to be the exact opposite of each other, but in fact they are a continuous circuit. What they are pointing to is recognition of patterns. Each story type has its own set of structural patterns, and these invite certain ways of revealing them, certain sequences and timings, certain kinds of events and characters. If you grasp the underlying patterns of your basic story type, it's possible to ring changes in the methods of revelation, alter timings and sequences, introduce unexpected events and characters or omit some, for example; these changes refresh the story and keep the audience engaged. The tension and surprise that delight an audience are produced as much by their recognition of the games you are playing with the patterns that they know belong to the type, as by their recognition of the story type itself.

But there is another point to consider in these two statements, and that is the extent to which you can alter, or extend, the story itself by changing storytelling patterns. In Chapter 1, I suggested that you need to understand what your play is really 'about'. You need to understand what is the nature of the communication you want to have with your audience. To put it another way, you need to know what is the story you are telling.

GOLDILOCKS AND THE THREE BEARS: THE REWRITE

An example: in workshops, fairy tales can serve as a basis for storytelling improvisation. Because we all know the tales so well, improvisers often respond very differently to the structure of the tale and its familiar details. Some feel them to be restrictive and want to take them apart. Others feel that they provide security, and want to play with the surface of the tale, with the vocabulary of the dialogue, or the tone. Generally, everyone seems to want to use the familiarity of the tales to demonstrate his storytelling virtuosity.

In one version of *Goldilocks and the Three Bears*, four improvisers presented the tale as a 'reality tv' crime report. The three bears were being interviewed in a television studio by a reporter about the break-in at their house. As with the usual type of such shows (*Crimewatch*, for example), the interviewer seemed sympathetic, setting out to elicit details of the crime that would enable the perpetrator to be caught. The tone, initially, was ironic, because – of course – we all knew who the 'perpetrator' was. But in the course of the improvisation, the interview shifted ground; the reporter began to attack the bears for their irresponsible carelessness in leaving their house unlocked (in this day and age!), and to sneer at their eating habits and home furnishings. The bears immediately became

defensive, trying to justify their tastes and behaviour, and struggled (fruitlessly) to return the interview to its original purpose. They found themselves suddenly, and alarmingly, switched from the position of victims of a home invasion to that of social undesirables. The ironic tone of the first few moments turned on its head, and became instead rather cruel and dark. The audience became very quiet, picking up on the uneasiness.

When the improvisation ended, I asked the quartet what story they felt they had been telling: *Goldilocks and the Three Bears*, they said. I asked the audience what story they felt they had been told. They had heard and seen a story about scapegoats, outsiders, social exclusion and bullying; one person said she thought it was about race. All were agreed that this story had spoken about the unpalatable ways in which societies deal with those who are in some way different. The improvisers were astonished. Wasn't it *Goldilocks and the Three Bears*? Many of the details were there, though Goldilocks was – crucially – missing, substituted by a slick TV reporter instead. And the location had changed, from the bears' house to the TV studio. The group deliberated: what else had changed, to make such a difference?

Eventually they decided it was the point of view that had altered. The fairy tale is usually told from a point of view closely aligned with Goldilocks. We go with her as she finds the house open, creeps in, eats the porridge because she's hungry (and so on), and we share her worry about the return of the bears because she is a little human child and bears are dangerous to humans. This new version had a different point of view. Goldilocks was missing, so it wasn't hers. But nor was it told from the bears' point of view. Whose point of view, then, was governing the storytelling? 'Goldilocks's kind.' someone said; 'Us. Not the bears' kind.' It was a very perceptive answer.

By shifting the point of view, the improvisers had created another, altogether deeper, level of story.

So was it *Goldilocks and the Three Bears?* In many respects it still was; but the tale had become the vessel for a much larger and darker communication with the audience. What was the story type the improvisers had employed, I asked? Everyone was agreed: the spider and the fly, in which a predator who is initially disguised (here, the reporter) sets a trap for unwary victims (the bears).

NEXT STEPS

Having thought about the extent to which you will be embedded within your play, and begun to explore the latent energy in potential ideas for plays through the discovery of dramatic metaphors, you now need to plan your storytelling. It's clear, both from *The Prisoner's Dilemma* and from the improvised rewrite of *Goldilocks*, that your choices will be highly influential upon the nature of your communication with your audience. The way you decide to tell the story may substantially alter the nature of the story you eventually tell.

Good plays, in the final analysis, rest upon the storytelling structure. You can have a lively idea, bursting with energy, but unless it is moulded around the strongest possible framework, it won't deliver its full potential. The following chapters will concentrate on storytelling. Four fundamental dramatic principles, which constitute the 'framework', will be explored in depth: movement, action, conflict and juxtaposition.

And to help you continue to think interrogatively, we'll be using six basic questions to gather and organize information:

- where?
- when?
- who?
- what?
- why?
- how?

THE SIX BASIC QUESTIONS

The craft of writing a stage play is, at heart, a matter of organizing a steady release of information to the audience. The six basic questions can be used throughout the process of planning and writing as category headings to remind you about the kinds of information you need to deliver. They are orientational and navigational aids for the audience:

Where? orientates us in space. It gives us the location of the story 'world', and as the play unfolds, it maps the world for us. The most basic level of information addresses issues of geography: a town, a country, or the layout of a house. From this, we learn how to navigate your use of onstage and offstage space throughout. *Where?* also addresses the culture of the story world: the kinds of lives which are lived within it, the types of people who live them, their ideas, beliefs and values. From this more complex level of information, we can determine the types of stories which will plausibly occur within the story world, and assess the progression of the story events.

When? orientates us in time. At its basic level, it places the story world within a historical moment that develops our understanding of the culture and its inhabitants. It gives us the duration of the story: a continuous narrative will take place over a short, concentrated period of time; an episodic story will deliver brief capsules of time spread over a long period. It orders the chronology of your story, allowing you to disrupt straightforward progression in your choice of storytelling method: we use when? to help us unravel your structure of flashbacks or simultaneous action and grasp the development of the story. And it organizes the relationship between the past, present and future, most particularly as these bear upon your characters.

Who? orientates us with regard to the characters who inhabit the space and time of your story world. It identifies the character hierarchy, so that we know which character you want us to follow, who will challenge, who will assist. It introduces us to the unique nature of each character: her personality, thoughts and feelings, as well as her material circumstances: sex, race, age, class, economic circumstances, and so on.

What? orientates us with regard to the story that unfolds. It addresses the nature of the events that happen to your characters in the space and time of the story world; the decisions that the characters make and their consequent deeds. What? shapes the forward movement of the story from beginning to end.

Why? orientates us with regard to the motivation of your characters and story. It may point to past events, before the play begins, to explain the underlying reasons for current events occurring, and for characters' individual reactions to them. It also enables us to predict possible future events and character responses.

How? orientates us within your storytelling method. It provides us with the map key to enable us to understand your organization of time and space, character and story. It releases the information we require in answer to where? when? who? what? and why? by means of two primary delivery systems: the visual (what is seen) and the aural (what is heard).

The Visual and Aural Toolkit

In a stage play, you have two sets of 'tools' at your disposal to deliver answers to the six basic questions.
   Visual tools:

- The stage itself
- Actor's facial expressions, gestures and movement
- Actor's costume, makeup and hairstyle
- Set
- Lighting
- Properties (personal objects such as a packet of cigarettes, or elements of the set, such as a table lamp).

Aural tools:

- Actor's spoken dialogue
- Actor's non-verbal utterances (coughs, screams, whistles, crying)
- Sound effects (dogs barking, gunfire, police sirens)
- Instrumental music
- Songs.

HOW? SEEING AND HEARING THE SIX QUESTIONS IN PERFORMANCE

The sixth question how? deploys the visual and verbal elements to pose, and answer, the other five questions.

Where? Set, properties, costume, makeup and hairstyle, and lighting provide a visual image of the story world. The stage layout creates visual boundaries between onstage and offstage space. Aurally, accents and speech idioms in dialogue also locate the story world, as can music and sound effects: a blues song suggests the Deep South, the rumble of city traffic, an urban location.

When? Set, properties, costume, makeup and hairstyle visually render historical period. Lighting suggests time of day, or season. Changes of set, costume and lighting, signal transitions in time. Lighting and darkness ('blackouts') signal the beginnings and endings of scenes. Aurally, archaic vocabulary and carefully chosen sound effects (a railway steam engine, for example), can indicate a period setting, while music can signal scene transitions.

Who? Dialogue and non-verbal utterances address character aurally, in tandem with the visual signs of facial expression, gesture and movement, costume, makeup and hairstyle. Set, properties and lighting communicate who? visually in the juxtaposition between character and environment. Music and song can signal a character's emotional state.

What? Dialogue tells us what's happening; visually, we are shown via physical actions (facial expressions, gesture, movement). Sound effects can also communicate what? (a gunshot, a car crash), as can alterations in costume, makeup and hairstyle (a ripped shirt, smeared lipstick, dishevelled hair). Lighting effects (a flash of lightning) can reveal what?, whilst shadow and darkness can conceal it.

Why? Dialogue and non-verbal utterances convey motivation aurally; facial expression, gesture and movement, visually. A key property can also serve as a visual carrier of why? (In Ibsen's *Hedda Gabler*, Hedda's sexual revulsion is expressed by burning her ex-lover's book. To her (and to him), it's his 'child'.)

With the six questions primed to gather and sort your raw material, and the visual and aural toolkit at your disposal to convey the answers, your next step is to begin to structure your play.

3 THE FIRST PRINCIPLE: MOVEMENT

I've spoken about movement in the context of the potential energy of an idea, and in relation to distance and audience engagement. In both those instances, the term has been employed as a metaphor to encourage you to 'write out' – the process of transfer (literally, moving your play) from your mind to the page or computer screen. It wasn't a random metaphor: movement is one of the fundamental principles of drama.

CHANGING POSITIONS

It's also very familiar. We are well used to observing motion, and to being in motion ourselves. We're accustomed to movement both in and through space, and in and through time; and we're also used to movement occurring both externally and internally. Ideas and feelings shift ground within us (remember Abi Morgan in Chapter 2: 'I've moved on in the year since I wrote that.') just as our limbs and muscles do when we shift our physical ground. Even when we are still, there's a tremendous amount of muscle activity going on, just to maintain our position. When we think about movement, we think of going from somewhere to somewhere else; and to achieve this transition, energy must be expressed in a given direction.

In drama, movement is a core element of the structures of story and character. When we talk about the progression of a story, the arc or journey of a character, reversals of fortune,

revelations, or about sequences and moments, movement is what we're really describing: movement that brings about change.

The critic Tzvetan Todorov uses a different term: 'transformation'. He describes five stages of transformation that a situation undergoes in the course of a certain kind of story. At the beginning, a state of balance exists; then something occurs to tip the situation off-balance. The situation is then in motion – perhaps we could think of it as 'falling', as we do when we lose our balance. (It need not be falling only in a negative sense: there is also 'falling in love' or 'falling on your feet', by which we mean having some good luck. However, there is 'falling flat on your face', 'falling down on the job' and 'falling over each other' to remind us of the downside.) The situation will continue to move – to fall – until someone recognizes that the original balance has been lost, and tries to repair or restore it. At the end, balance is once again achieved, but it is rarely exactly the same balance as at the outset. The new balance may appear to be very similar, but it is always different in at least one crucial respect: it is 'after the fall'.

MOVEMENT IN SPACE

Movement implies change. If we think in spatial terms again, we can identify three planes of movement: vertical (up/down), horizontal (left/ right) and in depth (forwards/ backwards). Loss of balance often involves a

Balance

We tend to use 'balance' as a positive term in our everyday vocabulary, even an ideal: we speak admiringly of people who have balanced judgement. But physical balance can be a very fragile state: it depends what you're trying to balance on. Insecure ground undermines balance immediately, and makes us nervous of our footing; the 'even keel' of our emotions also becomes fragile. Think, too, about how wobbly a belief can become when confronted with a powerful counter-argument. Yet, with our feet on solid ground, our faith in something secure, our balance is very strong. But so too is the balance of an experienced sailor on the deck of a ship. Though the ground underfoot is apt to shift, the sailor's balance is attuned to it and is flexible, adaptable. Often, as the inexperienced sailor finds to her cost, it is rigidity, incapacity to adapt, that makes balance unsustainable in adverse circumstances. 'Balance' is another valuable metaphor: it allows us to think about context, complementarity and contrast, and about motion and stillness, each located within the physical, intellectual and emotional dimensions of character and story.

yourself, having tripped over something minute in public, making a large show of examining the – almost invisible – culprit, to demonstrate to anyone who might be observing that you are the victim of hostile circumstances rather than hopelessly drunk or incompetent? We tend to do this because the trip makes us feel foolish, and we wish to reassert our sense of self-respect along with our upright position.)

It's valuable to think in physical terms like this, for your play will eventually transfer from the page into these same three spatial planes on stage. Though your characters and story will be fictional – even if you are writing a biographical play, it will still be fictionalised – your actors will be solidly real, and they will be moving around within the real space of the physical stage, which has height, width and depth. So if you can think of the movement of your story in physical terms – as movement – it can help you understand how to translate that into the kinds of stage directions for the director, designer and actor that express the development of the story accurately. Literally, you will be able to translate your story into action. (We will explore writing stage directions in detail in Chapter 7.)

Let's look at two ways in which movement in story and character can be generated:

- character status reversal
- revelation and discovery

movement on the vertical plane (we fall down), but it can also involve, at the same time, movement on the horizontal plane (falling to the side) and on the depth plane (we fall backwards or forwards). When we get up again, we are often spatially not quite where we were before; and our internal perspective has also changed, along with our external position. (For example, have you ever found

CHARACTER STATUS REVERSAL – WHAT IS STATUS?

EXERCISE
What do you think I mean by 'status'? How do we attribute status to a person in our society? Make some notes about this.

A Status Checklist

- Class
- Sex and gender
- Race
- Ethnic origin
- Religious creed
- Age
- Possession/lack of wealth
- Employment
- Education
- Membership of groups or parties
- Fame/ notoriety
- Personal qualities

Go through the list and under each heading, think of high status and low status examples.

COMMENTS

Did you notice that you probably started to think in terms of high or low status? For example, in Britain the class system still grips us, and an (often unspoken) assumption is made that members of one social class are inherently of higher status than members of another. Certainly we still see many examples of that assumption being played out in terms of the privileges and opportunities available to different groups. So status as a term implies a position on an ascending or descending scale.

Some categories are less contentious than others. Education and employment are relatively easy: we tend to assume, in our society, that highly educated people are of higher status than the uneducated, and that the employed have higher status than the unemployed. And within employment, some jobs are widely held to confer higher status than others: think of the different ways in which we tend to talk about a doctor and a supermarket shelf-filler, for example.

But others aren't at all easy. This may be because the attribution of status differs very acutely depending upon your point of view, and there is a lot of heated social debate surrounding it. For example, are men higher status than women? Or the reverse? Your answer may well depend on whether you are male or female! But you may also find it hard to say whether men *in general* are higher or lower status than women *in general*; you can probably think of some men who are higher, but others who are definitely lower, and so on. So you may find yourself wanting to be specific to individual cases, and to take into account other factors.

VALUE JUDGEMENTS

But another reason why attributing high/ low status may be quite difficult is because the attempt makes us aware that, when we speak of status, we may – whether intentionally or not – be signalling value judgements: that 'high status' people are somehow better or more valuable than 'low status' people. And this realization can make us feel rather uncomfortable. Consider, for example, how fraught it is to attribute high/low status under the categories of race or religious creed. Yet in our society it is undeniable that historically we have acted out, and do still act out, these contentious distinctions throughout our social systems.

It can make us feel uncomfortable, in societal terms, because we know that this underlying implication of worth deeply affects the kinds of opportunities available; it can render people powerful or powerless, for example, and can allow or preclude the possibility of change (or movement). We can be made additionally uncomfortable by the recognition that each is dependent upon the other for its definition: in order to be 'high status', you must have people below you; in order to be 'low status', you must have people above you. And further, if you are going to try to change your status, you must bring about a reciprocal change in someone else's: for one person to rise, another has to fall in relative terms, to maintain the distinction between the two. If, however, you wish to maintain your status, you need others also to maintain theirs relative to you, which may mean you have to block their movement in either direction, by preventing either their rise or their fall; if you rise, you must take them up with you, if you fall, you cannot afford to fall alone. So, as with the notion of 'falling' itself, you can also think of status change in both positive and negative ways.

Stage characters are highly developed embodiments of these status distinctions, and their spheres of dramatic activity turn upon their movement along the status scale from high to low or low to high. Stage characters therefore achieve a great deal of their power to provoke the debate between you, your play and your audience by means of activating the discomforts we feel about the subtextual value judgements implicit in status. Character status goes to the very heart of the argument of a play, and thus will form a key element in constructing the communication you wish to have with your audience.

STATUS REVERSAL IN *THE SERVANT*

Let's return to *The Servant*, to see how status reversal drives a dramatic story and can exploit subtextual value judgements to provoke an audience. Tony and Barrett are examples of one of the most frequently recurring status pairs in drama – master and servant. Tony (the master) is young, handsome, privileged, with a private income.

How Does Status Change Occur?

It can happen in large or small ways; it can be triggered internally within a character, or externally, by another character or by an outside occurrence; and it can be precipitated on any or all of the three human levels – the physical, the intellectual and the emotional. Some examples:

- Goliath (high status) is hit by a stone from David's (low status) sling (external, by another character) (physical level). Goliath is killed (very low status!) and David becomes a hero (high status). (Large change)
- I (low status) finally work out (intellectual level, internal) how to reset all the page margins on my (high status) computer. My status rises, having now conquered the machine, which thus falls in status relative to me. (Small change, though not to me!)
- An office worker (low status) who is being bullied by a supervisor (high status) summons up the courage (internal, emotional level) to confront the offender, who backs down. The supervisor's status falls relative to the office worker, whose status rises. (Small change)

Change is brought about by a physical action in David and Goliath's case, while the office worker's change is probably achieved through verbal means. So status can be changed through language as well as by physical actions.

Barrett (the servant) has none of those advantages. At the outset of the play, Tony is the high status character, Barrett the low. The arc of the story is the contrary movement each character makes from his initial status to its opposite. Though Barrett is still, in employment terms, the servant at the end of the play – Tony still pays his wages – he is, in status terms, now the master. Tony, though still Barrett's employer, by the end of the play, is obeying Barrett's orders.

If we consider this movement pattern of Tony's and Barrett's in terms of the three planes, it's obvious that there is huge movement on the vertical plane, as 'high' and 'low' imply. This transition from high to low/ low to high status is a basic unit of movement in drama. It provides the development – literally, the forward movement – of the story, and thus gives you an invaluable structural tool: status reversal helps to shape each scene of your play, within the escalating reversals of the whole story.

But in dramatic terms, Tony's fall and Barrett's rise wouldn't be so disturbing to a modern audience if it only involved movement on the vertical plane. As in life, movement often occurs in more than one plane at once, so it is necessary in drama to orchestrate some lateral movement, too, and some alteration in relative depth. Neil Bartlett's adaptation achieves this very well by developing the characters beyond the simple boundaries of their status roles, giving them a kind of psychosexual interdependence which means that, by the end of the play, it is really not clear who is entirely master and who is entirely servant. For just as Barrett cleverly orchestrates Tony's downfall by pandering to his emotional as well as physical needs and desires, so it is clear that Tony's unthinking pliability also answers Barrett's own emotional needs and desires. Each man is, therefore, to a greater or lesser extent, in thrall to the other.

BACKGROUND, FOREGROUND AND MIDDLE GROUND

A servant could be conceived of as a 'background' character, hovering behind the 'foreground' character of the master. However, Barrett isn't a minor character – the play is, after all, called *The Servant*. But if we think of him in depth terms as 'background', we understand how he must operate: covertly rather than overtly. He can't command, he must subtly persuade and insinuate until the reversal is achieved. By the end, Barrett has stepped foward as Tony has stepped back.

In Neil Bartlett's staging, Barrett initially operated behind Tony, constantly upstage of him. By the mid-point, he was often downstage in the foreground, driving Tony upstage into the background. By the end, however, the two men sat side by side on a couch together, occupying a 'middle ground' position which was very disturbing to the audience (remember the comments about wanting 'to go home and take a shower'?) This side-by-side image implied a kind of mutuality between the two men, and the audience were uneasy about why this should be so. Hence: 'why does Barrett do it?', 'Why doesn't Tony stop it?' and 'What happens next to the characters?' Three questions provoked by the characters and story moving within all three planes.

THE FIVE STAGES OF TRANSFORMATION

If we look at *The Servant* according to the five-stage transformational model, we need to identify the initial condition of balance. Tony has just returned to England from several years in Africa; he has inherited money from his late father, which has enabled him to buy a little house in a fashionable part of town. But it's in a bit of a mess, and Tony isn't particularly energetic at sorting things out for himself. This is the opening state of affairs: Tony's in a rather pleasant situation, with lots of positive things about it. It is balanced but because of Tony's characteristic laziness, it isn't ideal, and thus it is ripe for change.

So Tony sets about changing things for the better by trying to alter the one thing that isn't ideal. He hires a manservant to take care of everything he can't be bothered to do himself. This is the second stage of the transformation: the occurence that disrupts the initial balance. What's nice here is that it is actually Tony who alters the balance. It isn't an outside event that forces the disruption, it is Tony's own choice. And indeed things do change, initially (in Tony's eyes) for the better. But Tony's friends become disturbed by Barrett's growing influence and Tony's acquiescence; in particular, they can see that it is actually bringing about a deterioration in his character (stage three). They frantically try to alert Tony to the problem, but he can't, or won't, see it; meanwhile Barrett, following his own agenda, increases his control over his master.

Eventually, despite the friends' attempts to defeat Barrett (stage four), the servant wins, and it is the friends who are got rid of. So the fifth stage, that restores balance, produces a distorted echo of the opening situation: where initially it was Barrett who entered as the disruptive element, the final inversion expels the 'disruptive' friends, and leaves a new balance of Tony and Barrett existing comfortably side by side. Comfortably, that is, for them, in Neil Bartlett's version of the outcome: the final balance is one with which both Tony and Barrett appear content, but as Jack Davenport's 'bombshell' remark acknowledged, it is not one with which the audience necessarily feels equally comfortable. The source of their discomfort is, of course, the stew of subtextual value judgements about class and especially, sexuality, that the status reversal brings to the surface.

SCRIPT EXERCISE

Choose a pair of characters and a situation from the list below. Write a short scene (between three and five pages) between the two characters, with dialogue and action.

To help you think about your scene, use the **Exercise Checklist** (page 44) either before you write, or after you've written your draft and are reviewing it.

Character pairs and situations:

- A father (or mother) and his/her fifteen-year-old daughter (or son). For the first time, s/he asks to stay out overnight at a friend's party.
- The owner of a pedigree breeding dog (or bitch) and the owner of the neighbourhood pooch. Who has done what to whom...?
- A bookie and a punter who is trying to place a bet. It's the very last moment before the race starts.
- 'Me and my shadow/ walkin' down the avenue...'.
- Two turkeys on Christmas Eve (or Thanksgiving). The clock's ticking....

(If none of these pairs appeals, choose a pair and a situation you would like to play with. But ensure, in your situation, that something's got to give, and that one or other of the pair is going to have to give it.)

Don't try to cram too many things into the first attempt. You can keep returning to this exercise as many times as you wish, trying new things each time. For your first go, concentrate simply on making the two characters move their status positions relative to one another. As you try it again, you can introduce other elements, making the reversal subtler, the characters more detailed and vivid, perhaps the tone completely different, the scene longer with more than one reversal.

Exercise Checklist

- Who is high status and who is low status at the beginning of the scene? By the end, their positions will have been reversed.
- Why is one character higher status than the other? What is it that makes him/her so? What makes the high status character vulnerable to 'falling'? What would make him/her 'lose balance'? That's the weakness the low status character exploits in order to raise his/ her own status.
- What is the state of affairs at the beginning of the scene? (Opening balance)
- What occurs to disturb this? (Disruption) Why does it occur? Is it an occurrence on (primarily) the physical, intellectual or emotional level?

- Is the change triggered internally or externally to the characters? (Externally might be the arrival of a letter, or someone's Lottery numbers coming up, for example)
- How does the character who wants to change status set about achieving this goal?
- When does someone notice the change? What makes him/her notice it? (Recognition)
- What does s/he do to try to restore the balance and regain status? (Attempt to repair)
- What is the final state of affairs? What are the new status positions? (new balance)
- Has the movement been simply a fall/rise on the vertical scale, or have other things changed as well? What things?

COMMENTS
The most common problems with scenes of this kind are:

- Relative status isn't sufficiently clearly established at the outset. (Not enough thinking about why these two characters hold the status positions they do)
- The moment of reversal isn't clear, or reversal doesn't actually occur. (The nature of the disruption hasn't been thought through, or properly activated. No loss of balance)
- The reversal seems completely arbitrary and unbelievable. (The reason for the fall/rise isn't sufficiently rooted in character; too much reliance on outside factors that wouldn't plausibly happen to these people. Or turkeys.)
- The scene doesn't have a clear beginning and ending that make sense in terms of each other. (Not enough thought given to the structure of the story)

- It isn't clear what the story of the scene is really about. (What was the question which motivated it? If there wasn't one, the scene is just a technical exercise, in which the writer has little or no personal investment. S/he is 'absent'. Even at this simple level of story, try to involve yourself in the characters and their situation)

It's worth asking someone else to read the scene after you've written it, to see whether what they draw from it is what you intended. If they don't pick up on something or go off in an unexpected direction, try to identify why this has occurred, and if you want to, rewrite the scene to make it deliver your intention better. But if they have drawn something unexpected from it, pause for a moment and consider: do you like what they came up with? Does it add another dimension to the scene? If so, keep it.

Breaking the 'rules'

There are no unbreakable rules in playwriting. You should feel completely free to break anything that sounds like a rule if you have something that you believe works better. Your audience will have the final say as to whether or not it does work, and they will certainly tell you which is the case. You are, after all, in this together.

REVELATION AND DISCOVERY – RECOGNITION

Status reversal is a fundamental structural tool in drama. It is rooted in classical Greek dramatic poetry, to which the majority of Western theatre looks for its origins and a great deal of its technique. In Greek drama, the term *peripeteia* means reversal of fortune, and it is clear that the key word in terms of movement is reversal, a substantial alteration in the direction of movement. Another Greek device for creating movement is *anagnorisis*: recognition. I'm going to talk about it here in terms of revelation and discovery.

I have spoken a great deal about the extent to which your play will draw upon your worldview and your own ideas, hopes, fears and passions. In Chapter 2, I used emotive terms such as 'self-exposure' and 'give yourself away' to describe the process of writing, and pointed to the extent to which you will be embedded within your play. And I have suggested using maieutics – dynamic questions – as a means of uncovering your own personal relationship to the story itself throughout your planning and writing of it.

It should be apparent now that I've been describing the creation of a play as a continuous process of revelation, discovery, recognition and acknowledgement, a process that is reciprocal between playwright and audience. This is an arc of movement that bridges the separate space between stage and auditorium (if they are indeed separated) as the play also moves through the time it takes to perform it.

The Winter's Tale

Movement on the emotional level produces physical effects, too. In the climax of Shakespeare's *The Winter's Tale*, Leontes, whose insane jealousy sixteen years previously drove him to destroy his oldest friendship, his marriage and family, stands before a statue of Hermione, the wife he believes long dead. He has long since repented the enormity of his crimes against those he should most have trusted. Struck to the heart by the statue of Hermione not as she appeared sixteen years ago, but as she would look now had she lived, Leontes wants only to touch it – and then the statue moves, steps down to him from its pedestal. A magical restoration to life or a ruse whereby Hermione never died but instead remained sequestered for sixteen years? It doesn't matter which, for the truth of the moment is in the emotional force of Leontes' – and our – discovery that Hermione is alive and restored to him and to the daughter he (and she) believed lost.

The statue coming to life reminds us of the Greek myth of Orpheus, who descended into the Underworld to retrieve his dead wife Eurydice, and then lost her again through a fatal error. Leontes' joy at regaining what he had lost by his own foolishness makes us yearn for the same blessing. But we weep when we recognize that, whilst it may be attainable in myth, in life it is rarely so.

SELF-RECOGNITION: *OEDIPUS THE KING*

In Greek drama, the most powerful form of *anagnorisis* was self-recognition: the discovery of one's own true nature, for good or ill. The foremost classical example of this form of self-recognition is that of Oedipus in Sophocles's *Oedipus the King*. The great warrior-king of Thebes has sent his brother-in-law, Creon, to the Oracle of Apollo to discover why his city is suffering from famine and blight. Apollo's answer comes back: the cause is an unpurged crime: the ancient murder of Thebes' former king, Laius. Oedipus vows to discover and punish the murderer, to purify the city. He sends for the blind seer, Teiresias, to help him, but the old man evades his questions. Angrily, Oedipus threatens and accuses Teiresias, provoking him to reveal shocking news: Oedipus himself is the murderer. The king is outraged! He vows to uncover and smash what is clearly a conspiracy to overthrow him, cooked up by Teiresias and Creon.

It had been prophesied many years before that the son of King Laius would one day kill his father and marry his mother, Queen Jocasta. In an attempt to escape their fate, Laius and Jocasta had tried to destroy the child, but unbeknown to them, the baby had been rescued and taken abroad. In the course of time, the young warrior Oedipus, travelling towards Thebes, fell into a roadside brawl with an older man and killed him. Arriving in the city, he found it in turmoil following the death of its king; he stepped into the breach, united the city and cemented its stability by marrying the king's widow. And now, years later still, Thebes is on the brink of disaster once more.

Apollo's Oracle sets in train a series of revelations and recognitions: the older man he killed by the roadside was his father, Laius; the widowed queen he married, by whom he now has four children, is his own mother, Jocasta.

And the biggest revelation of all: Oedipus discovers who he himself is – until this point he did not know that he was himself the rescued baby, the Theban prince. In discovering his true identity, he finds that he has also fulfilled his inevitable destiny, and must now complete it by living up to his oath to lift the curse on the kingdom.

Beautiful Thing

Self-recognition is still the most potent form of discovery: the quest for true identity is a major dramatic theme in contemporary writing. In Jonathan Harvey's *Beautiful Thing*, sixteen-year-olds Jamie and Ste find out what kind of people they really are when they fall in love. Awkwardly for them in the conventional world they inhabit, it is each other they fall in love with, rather than girls. But Harvey's is not simply a play about discovering one's sexual orientation; it is about the ways in which we come to know ourselves best by the quality of the connections we make with other people. Jamie and Ste don't just find out that they are gay; they learn how to negotiate the difficult path between feeling and expressing love and care for another. Written in 1993, *Beautiful Thing* found a very wide audience, both male and female, gay and straight, because it turned upon this essentially human discovery.

MOVEMENT FROM 'LACK' TO 'GAIN'

The movement pattern implicit in the process of revelation, discovery, recognition and acknowledgement is a movement from ignorance to knowledge, or from innocence to experience. Underlying both those expressions is the same premise: a transition from a state that might be described as a 'lack' (lack of knowledge, lack of experience) to a state of 'possession' or 'gain', from not having to having. And there is an unspoken assumption that this is a good thing: we live in a society that deems the condition of not having to be generally undesirable. So the motivating force, dramatically, as socially, is the drive to acquire, to get.

But as we considered earlier in the case of 'falling', there is ambiguity here. Innocence is often regarded as an idealized state: foregoing one's innocence is deemed 'loss', whilst the undoing of another's state of innocence is often discussed in terms of 'corruption', 'theft' or 'ruin', all of which have very negative moral connotations. Even ignorance – a less idealized term than innocence – can still be 'blissful'. So it's necessary to set alongside the assumed positive pattern of movement from lack to gain, a recognition that in certain circumstances, the pattern is reversed: from gain to loss, and that this movement pattern is a possible negative. And most interestingly of all, we recognize that at its most complex, the pattern moves in both directions simultaneously, and is both positive and negative: in gaining the one we lose the other. In losing the beauty of innocence, we gain the ambiguity of experience. In gaining knowledge, we may lose the lack of responsibility ignorance conferred upon us.

MOVEMENT IN *OEDIPUS THE KING*

Status reversal was identified primarily as a transition on the vertical plane. But the most absorbing forms of movement are those which happen also on the horizontal and depth planes as well. Discovery – most especially self-revelation – offers a means of orchestrating movement in those other two planes. If we consider the example of Oedipus again, it's clear that at the outset of the play his status is about as high as it's possible to be: he is a hero king, the saviour of Thebes. By the end of the play he is an outcast, blinded by an act of appalling self-inflicted violence. The tremendous fall in status is apparent: he is now the lowest of the low.

But he didn't set out to change his status, and nor did anyone else in the play set out either to lower his status or to raise their own (as Barrett unquestionably did, in *The Servant*.) Oedipus' fall is brought about by his quest for information, that is, by his attempt to move laterally, from ignorance to knowledge. And notice that he sets out only to answer one particular question: why is the city cursed? He does not expect the answer to have any bearing upon himself, only to provide him with a focus for further action. But the Oracle's revelation, we might say, literally comes out of left field: in answering his specific question it does indeed move him laterally from ignorance to knowledge, but it also reveals unlooked-for information about himself, and thus changes his perspective (movement in the plane of depth.)

To trace this multidimensional pattern of movement, we can use the transformational model to help us.

EXERCISE
From my description above, make some notes in response to these questions:

- What is the initial state of affairs at the outset of the play? (the opening balance)
- What is the action or occurrence that disrupts this balance?
- Why does this action or occurrence happen?
- Who recognizes that a disruption has occurred, or is in the process of occurring?
- What happens next?

- What is the final state of affairs? (the new balance)

COMMENTS

The Opening Balance

The initial state of affairs is terrible. Thebes is in the grip of famine and blight, and its people are starving. They cannot understand why this is happening. They look to their idolized hero-king Oedipus to solve the puzzle and rescue them as he has done before. Though this is a bad state of affairs, it is still the opening balance: it is the ongoing condition at the outset of the play. But because it is a bad situation, we can see that it contains a need for change: it is a balance ripe for disruption, in the dramatic sense.

The Disruptive Element

The Oracle's answer is the disruptive element. By pointing to the cause of the pollution of the city, it sets in motion the 'detective story', to find the murderer and purge the crime.

Unbalancing the Opening Situation

The disruption occurs because Oedipus seeks to move from ignorance to knowledge (lateral movement). It's a high status act – the act of a king – but it is the act that will precipitate his fall. So in deliberately seeking this lateral movement, Oedipus not only tips the opening situation off-balance and into free-fall, he also, without recognizing that he is doing so, tips himself off his high-status balance. The question is, should he have done it? But how else was he to solve the puzzle and help his people?

Recognition of the Disruption

Since the Oracle's answer is delivered in public, everyone hears what is said, and also hears Oedipus vow to track down the killer. So everyone knows that a disruption has occurred; but since the true nature of the crime lies buried deep in Thebes' – and Oedipus' – history, there are very few who know the full extent of the disruption triggered by the Oracle's answer. There are, however, people who know pieces of the puzzle (his mother/wife Jocasta, the rescuers of the baby, for example) and one man who knows it all: Teiresias. When Oedipus summons him for information, Teiresias warns him not to proceed; it is only Oedipus' arrogance, in accusing Teiresias himself of complicity in the original crime that provokes the blind man into revealing the key information of Oedipus' guilt.

Oedipus' Fall

What happens next is that Oedipus rejects the answer and immediately accuses Teiresias of treason; and he widens the accusation to embrace his brother-in-law Creon. He crosses over, therefore, in his own eyes, from simply investigating an old murder to fighting to avert political overthrow. But he's wrong – that isn't what is happening at all. The irony is that the full nature of the old crime, once revealed, will itself cause his fall, without anyone else's help. So Oedipus' status begins to reverse at the moment Creon returns with the Oracle's answer: the moment his transition from ignorance to knowledge begins is also the moment of fall. Oedipus' fall begins at that precise moment because the Oracle's answer sets in train the discovery of who he truly is: the subject of a terrible prophecy which has, unwittingly, already been fulfilled. In seeking to exchange his ignorance of the cause of Thebes' problems for knowledge, Oedipus loses also an ignorance of his own origins which we might term 'blissful'. It is a splendid example of the ambiguity of loss/gain. In learning about the truth of his past, Oedipus gains a different kind of depth perspective upon his present condition.

The New Balance

The new balance is perhaps even more terrible than – but also as ambiguous as – the opening. It is also an inversion of the opening balance. There, Thebes was in crisis; now, the curse is lifted and the city can move forward again. But, then, Oedipus was its powerful and revered king; now, he is a blinded exile, an untouchable. So the city has gained its survival but lost its monarch, with the concomitant risk of future political instability. Oedipus has his answer but also a new, unlooked-for identity and an uncertain future.

RELEASING INFORMATION

As we can see from this example, the sequential process of revelation, discovery, recognition and acknowledgement is a means of structuring the storytelling. Notice that it is a time-based sequence: we cannot recognize and acknowledge what has not yet been revealed and discovered. Structuring your story is actually about timing the release of information, orchestrating the method of release and deciding to whom within the story it will be released; that is, unless the information is to be revealed to the audience but withheld from the characters (which creates irony). So there are three questions you will need to keep asking yourself:

- To whom is each piece of information revealed? (Character? Audience? Character + audience?)
- How is it revealed to him/her (and/or us)?
- When is it revealed? (To us at the same time as the character? Before? After?)

But of course, you can't answer any of those questions until you have fully understood what story you're telling your audience (the nature of the communication you wish to have with them.) The story you're telling will

The Value of 'Prior Knowledge'

Understand what it is your audience already knows. Telling them unnecessary information isn't revelation, it's redundancy; it undermines tension, destroys pace and energy, and bores them. In good plays, they begin to predict what's coming next and how and when. Anticipate what they'll predict, and then you can decide to:

- Deliver their expectation
- Deliver it, but vary the timing – sooner or later than they expect it
- Deliver it from an unexpected quarter, or by unexpected means of revelation
- Not deliver it.

These choices form part of your storytelling method, generating the pace, rhythm, energy and tension of your play that keeps the audience on the hook.

Alongside 'What does the audience already know?', determine what each character already knows. It should be different for each character since possession/lack of information is frequently the cause of a status reversal.

determine the nature of the information that is to be revealed step by step, the direction of its movement, and its timing.

USING OPPOSITES

Clearly you don't want to give away all your information in one go at the outset – otherwise there's no play! So you're going to be thinking not only in terms of revelation but also of concealment; not only discoveries but also secrets. And this leads us to think of what might be the opposites of recognition and acknowledgement: the failure to recognize, and (perhaps) the refusal to acknowledge. If you think about *Oedipus the King* in these terms, then it is easy to identify what is secret (Oedipus' real history), that it has deliberately been concealed (by Laius and Jocasta), and the consequences of that decision to conceal. Had his true nature been revealed to Oedipus years previously, the tragedy would probably not have occurred. But we can also see the interplay of recognition and failure to recognize: Oedipus is warned by Teiresias not to ask who Laius' murderer is (recognition of danger by Teiresias) but Oedipus fails to recognize the value of the warning (because he does not not know who he truly is). Once the truth is revealed, a pivotal moment arises: does he acknowledge it, or refuse to do so? Whichever he does, there will be enormous consequences, for himself, his family and the people of Thebes.

SCRIPT EXERCISE

Look at the three pictures (Figs 5–7). The setting is the Millennium Dome in London. In Fig. 5, A is making a telephone call. In Fig. 6, A is sharing fast food with B. In Fig. 7, C is showing B a small piece of paper. Both the telephone and the piece of paper are potential means of revealing information (or concealing it, if it is incorrect, incomplete or sends someone off on a wild goose chase).

Based on the pictures, write a short scene (three to five pages) in which two of the characters share a secret that is unknown to the third character. In the course of the scene, the audience should discover what the secret is; it's up to you whether or not the third character also discovers it.

- I have called the characters A, B and C, but this doesn't necessarily mean that C is the

Figure 5   Exterior: The Millennium Dome, London: Character A.

Figure 6   Interior: Fast-food restaurant: Characters A and B.

Figure 7   Exterior: The Dome: Characters B and C.

third character (the one who doesn't know the secret). It's just easier for me to refer to them this way, without predetermining their names. You should give them names, to help you think of them as people, not just ciphers for the purpose of the exercise.

- Though the pictures are numbered sequentially (this is for printing and for reference purposes), you can reorder the sequence in any way you like, for your scene.

Pictures can be a very useful stimulus for story ideas. But if these three pictures don't interest you, devise your own three characters and write a scene fulfilling the same brief, as above. Alternatively, you might like to find your own set of pictures to stimulate the exercise, perhaps from a newspaper or magazine.

As with the status reversal exercise, this one is also an exercise to which you can keep returning. The same advice about over-complication in the first attempt also applies; concentrate first on the process of revelation, discovery, recognition and acknowledgement. And as before, ask someone to read the scene after you've written it: you want to know whether they got the information as required, or too early/too late, and so on.

COMMENTS
The most common problems with these scenes tend to be:

- We can't tell what the information being revealed to us actually is. (Not enough thinking about the story of the scene)
- We don't understand why the revelation matters, or to whom it matters. (The story isn't sufficiently rooted in character)
- No-one appears to recognize or acknowledge the revelation – or if this is an ironic scene, it's not clear why they fail/refuse to do so. (Ditto)

Exercise checklist

Keep in mind the opposite pairs:

- revelation/concealment (you could also think of this as a disguise, lie or trick)
- discovery/secret
- recognition/failure to recognize (accidental or deliberate)
- acknowledgement/refusal to acknowledge.

As you decide the information to be revealed, the method of revelation and the timing, consider:

- what do we (the audience) already know?
- what do they (the characters) already know?
- why isn't the information already known? (Perhaps because it refers to something that has not yet happened; or because it has been concealed/is a secret; or it is known but is not being recognized/acknowledged.)

- The information is obviously something we already know. (Not enough thinking about the audience's prior knowledge)
- The information is obviously something the character/s already know, and they are only 'revealing' it to each other for our benefit. (Not enough thinking about character relationships and prior knowledge. It produces a phenomenon drily referred to as 'first act amnesia', where characters appear (conveniently) to have forgotten even the most basic information about each other and their situation)
- There are no apparent consequences to the revelation and discovery, or we cannot

predict any likely consequences to be forthcoming later. (No real story, no clear beginning and ending to the scene)

- The scale of the revelation seems to be out of proportion to the characters and their apparent situation. (Story not properly rooted in character; the stakes- what is to be won or lost – are set too high or too low)
- There doesn't seem to be a story to the scene (What was the question that drove the scene?)

Remember that this exercise is part of an exploration of movement (that is, about change): did things change, in your scene, as a result of the revelation and discovery? In particular, did the revelation and discovery alter characters' status relative to each other? In future versions of this exercise, you could concentrate on the interaction between the two: the ways in which knowledge/ignorance confers/ withholds status, and especially, the consequences, in status terms, of the movement between the two conditions. Loss or gain? Fall or rise? Does it lead to a change in perspective?

WARM-UP EXERCISES OR WRITER'S RESCUE

The two script exercises in this chapter could be compared to a pianist's finger-flexing exercises. But they are also akin to an artist's rough sketches in preparation for a big painting: a way of trying out a little fine detail. Use them for both purposes when you're writing your play. Since they both address very basic aspects of story structure, they can give you little models as reminders for scenes in your play.

But one of their best uses can be to help you solve a problem with a scene that's going nowhere, or that you can't seem to get started. Playing with status and revelation can help release the blockage. So if you're warming up, trying something out, or stuck in a rut, these exercises are useful additions to your writer's toolkit.

4 THE SECOND PRINCIPLE: ACTION

'ACTION' IN FILM AND THEATRE

In film-making, as the camera begins to roll, the actors are cued to start by the call 'Action'. But what does the term actually mean? In the cinema, we are used to it appearing as a description of genre: an 'action movie', or as one element of a hybrid genre – 'action-adventure', 'action-comedy'. We are also used to hearing some films and television shows described as being 'action-packed'. When you hear a drama described this way, what do you expect to see and hear? What do you expect not to see and hear? Pause for a moment, and note down your thoughts about this.

You may have noted that you expect lots of physical activity, and big set-pieces such as car chases or fights or explosions, with plenty of accompanying noise and spectacle. You probably don't expect to see long periods of stillness with characters talking quietly at length – and especially not periods of looking at a silent image. 'Action', in this sense, seems to imply a rapidly escalating succession of events, images and sounds, tumbling over one another to create tremendous pace and narrative tension. Sometimes, despite the excitement generated, if that rapid momentum isn't sufficiently harnessed to the task of storytelling, the overall story, and particularly the individuality of the characters, can become lost in the flurry of activity.

Why don't we tend to describe stage or radio plays as 'action-packed', or employ 'action' as a specific type of theatre or radio play, do you think?

You might have said that if action implies car-chases and explosions, you can't do those on stage or radio. But why not? Particularly in radio, all that is required is the appropriate sound to conjure the specific mental images. Squealing tyres, booms and bangs (substantially the same kind of noisy soundtrack employed by a screen action sequence) are all very easy to produce. And sound effects of various kinds are also available in the theatre: if Shakespeare could have a massive storm onstage in *King Lear*, or the battle of Agincourt happening offstage in *Henry V* 400 years ago, then the theatre would have no difficulty in producing the illusion today. On screen, it is true, we can see the car-chases and explosions taking place, watch the rapid cutting from location to location that actually creates a lot of the pace and excitement; on stage and in radio drama, we must create the visual images in our imagination. But they can be invoked, given the right cues. Is this difference – the obscene of the visual element – sufficient reason?

COMPRESSION AND INTENSIFICATION

No, it isn't. Theatre is also a visual medium. (So, too, is radio, but in a different way.) The difference lies in the full spectrum of ways in which stories are first conceived, and then structured and delivered in theatre and radio as opposed to on screen. A significant difference lies in the much greater emphasis that theatre, in particular, places upon dramatic metaphor, which allows it to compress and intensify the scope of dramatic action. (Chapter 2 discusses compression in the 'latent energy' of an idea.)

In theatre, we compress the much larger flow of events down to a smaller, more dense series of images and sounds that carry a weight of meaning beyond the literal. In doing so, we affect the pace and rhythm of storytelling: whereas on screen the action sequence is usually fast-paced (because what we are seeing is really all we need to know at that moment), on stage the compressed metaphoric sequence of action needs time for us to unpack its range of meanings. So the rhythms and pace of a theatre play differ substantially from those of screenplays. That doesn't necessarily mean that all stage plays are slow-paced; variation in pace and rhythm is always needed, and often accelerates in the latter scenes. But in comparative terms, stage plays tend to have slower, more elongated, and often more complex rhythms than many screenplays do.

It's also sensible to observe here that you couldn't literally drive a couple of cars back and forth across the limited physical space of a theatre stage without looking rather daft! So the nature of stage action also differs from screen action because of what is appropriate to the fixed nature of stage space.

Theatre's greater emphasis on expression through dramatic metaphor actually benefits from the fixed nature of stage space: it supplies a strong set of physical boundaries that can be placed in counterpoint to the imaginary space of the story world. Imaginary space can embrace the confines of a small room (as in

Adaptation: stage space v. screen space

When stage plays are adapted for the cinema, the process of translation from stage space to screen space is often described as 'opening out' the story. This metaphor points to theatre's ability to compress action, but also implies, negatively, a sense of spatial 'cramping'. On stage, the play isn't cramped: spatial compression actually allows *time* – the pace and rhythms of the storytelling – to be treated more expansively. On screen, the same kind of spatial compression probably would appear cramped; screen stories require a more expansive use of *space*. The cinema's capacity to edit together images from this expanded space quickens the rhythm and pace of screen-storytelling, compressing time.

Ariel Dorfman's *Death and the Maiden*) or can span the globe, moving freely and immediately from Egypt to Rome and back again (as in Shakespeare's *Antony and Cleopatra*) on a character's say-so.

Compression and intensification are most effectively achieved through character, which tends to be much more strongly foregrounded in theatre. The degree of physical activity demanded is often reduced, and counterbalanced by a much greater degree of intellectual and emotional activity. Often, the latter forms find expression through language, but not solely; movement and gesture acquire heightened significance through interaction with dialogue. In some forms of physical theatre, there may be little or no spoken language; there, gesture and movement constitute a kind of language in themselves, addressing the activities of the mind and heart revealed entirely through the body. Action, through the medium of character, is often as much to do with what is going on internally, within a character, as externally.

DRAMATIC ACTION

So 'action' is very much more than a film genre or a descriptive label implying a kind of frenetic busyness. It is a fundamental structural principle in drama. When we use the term in this way, we are actually using a form of shorthand: what we mean is dramatic action, rather than simply physical activity. Keep this in mind, as we go on.

In the dictionary, action – as a general term – is defined as 'a process of working to produce alteration', 'a voluntary act or deed', 'an engagement (for example, between troops)', 'an expenditure of energy or influence', and 'an operating mechanism'. Synonyms for action might be: 'achievement', 'accomplishment', 'step' and 'undertaking'.

Do you recognize familiar aspects here? 'Working to produce alteration' echoes earlier consideration of movement producing change. 'An expenditure of energy' also echoes our thoughts about movement as the expression of energy in a given direction. Is dramatic action, then, simply synonymous with movement as considered in Chapter 3? Focus on the first part of the definition ('a process of working') and we can see how they might fit together: action is a *process* that generates movement designed to produce change. So status reversal, revelation and discovery (which orchestrate movement) are also to be understood as components of the process of action.

But notice something else of importance here. 'A process of working to produce alteration' implies both a structure and a goal or objective; it is not randomly occurring, it has order, direction and purpose. This helps us further with the linkage between action and movement. Movement could be random, disordered; it need not imply any innate purpose. Action, on the other hand, has an innate purpose, and this organizes movement, gives it focus and direction.

HUMAN AGENCY

The synonyms – achievement, accomplishment, step, undertaking – also remind us that action is something which is *done*. The term 'drama' derives from the Greek verb 'to do', meaning 'something which is done': so drama *is* action, by this light. And we can observe, in those four synonyms, an implication of human agency: people achieve, accomplish, undertake, take steps. This would underpin, in the dictionary definition, the 'voluntary' aspect of action, and also the notion of 'engagement' (a term we have used to describe the relationship between your play and your audience). What's being highlighted here is the key role played by human will and desire. If we understand dramatic action to be a purpose-driven process that generates movement designed to produce change, then the process begins because someone wants change to occur, decides to make it happen and acts accordingly.

The principle of action produced by human desire and will is the most powerful form of action in drama. It addresses, too, the fifth definition: 'an operating mechanism'. A character's desire and his will to satisfy it creates the operating mechanism by which action occurs, and also dictates how it will unfold. Let's acknowledge at once, though, that action (in the sense of events or happenings) can also occur outside the human level: in nature (the eruption of a volcano, a fire, a storm) or on the supernatural level (the divine, demonic or uncanny). It can occur apparently randomly by chance or accident, not subject to human decision – a letter fails to arrive, or your Lottery numbers come up, for example. But for your play, treat these non-human events and the appearance of randomness as valuable only when they cut across human actions (usually disruptively), and thereby demand new decisions. Those decisions struggle with the disruption to restore the direction of movement towards the original purpose. To express it in familar terms, they become valuable when they throw things off-balance, or conversely, when they fortuitously provide the means of regaining a balance that has already been lost.

Rooting the action of your play on the human level helps you anchor the story securely in your characters, which, in turn, calls to your aid the full range and power of the actor. It allows you to focus the directed patterns of dramatic movement around a series of *inter*actions between character and context – between character and situation – and as a series of *trans*actions between characters. The core of your play is therefore less likely to be a series of external events than it will be a series of human dealings, many of which will be quite small-scale and subtle, and which will require time to evolve towards their conclusion. This is also helpful in terms of creating plausible action, because you are able to ask yourself 'What would this person do?' in the given circumstances of your projected story. If you can't work out what your character might reasonably do, it may well be because you've accidentally proposed something no real person would do.

CAUSE AND EFFECT: THE ARC OF ACTION

The basic arc of dramatic action is a simple one: a character finds himself in a situation (that may or may not initially be of his own making) and reaches a decision about it; as a result, he carries out a series of incremental physical and verbal acts. These produce consequences that either advance or retard fulfilment of his decision. On the basis of these consequences, and taking into account any

---

A Sense of Scale

Thinking of the principle of action in terms of human agency gives you a sense of scale, which is important for stage plays. Unlike the experience of watching a film in a cinema where an actor's face and body are magnified to a much greater size than ours, on stage the actor's real physical presence means that her physical size matches ours. The sense of 'magnification' in watching a stage character comes from the density and richness of characterization that the writer and actor create together, and the degree of proximity that we're drawn into, rather than from any optical illusion. Compression of the scope of the character into the actor's physical boundaries increases its intensity.

We remain aware throughout of the human scale of the character; it's the things she does and the way we engage with her that produce the magnification. It's important to remember that when you're trying to create 'larger than life' characters – villains such as Shakespeare's Richard III, for example. Richard is not actually 'larger': he is our size – that's part of his attraction, it's why we recognize and identify with him. What is 'larger' is the string of outrageous acts he performs, and his intense relish for them.

external factors that may also have occurred, he takes a new decision, requiring further acts, and so on. This becomes a causal chain: a logical sequence of causes and effects, where something happens *because of* what went before. On the human level, it becomes a sequence of action and reaction.

It is this type of story Todorov was outlining in his five stages of transformation (balance, disruption, recognition, attempt to repair, new balance). The same causal pattern underpins our earlier explorations of status reversal, revelation and discovery. So cause and effect sequences as units of action help to generate the movement we require to bring about change. We can see, too, that each of these sequences might itself be regarded as a complete miniature arc of action, accumulating into larger patterns to produce the overall action of the play. And finally, we can see that the apparent randomness of action occurring outside the human scale – a storm, a heart attack, the wrath of the gods – is not really accurate. These events have their own causal chains that aren't necessarily part of the dramatic story you are telling; they may, quite literally, be unfolding 'offstage', coming 'onstage' only when they cut across human action.

ALTERNATIVES TO CAUSE AND EFFECT

Look again at the issues of purpose and direction, causality and human desire and will, for there are distinctions to be drawn. Action is a purpose-driven process focused towards the creation of change; structuring the action of your play will, therefore, invite you to work step by step through the logic of that process, creating each of those miniature sequences. Each step will move the story incrementally forward, drawing nearer and nearer to the delivery of the final state after

change has been completed. Todorov's transformational arc can now be recognized as an arc of action that advances by the operation of cause and effect.

But it is equally possible to move your dramatic story forward without relying on cause and effect logic. It will however entail a radically different kind of story and approach to character, and will engage the audience in a different kind of communication. Martin Crimp's 1997 play *Attempts on Her Life* offers us seventeen brief scenes ('scenarios') each of which addresses some aspect of Anne (the 'her' whose life is being discussed). Each scene is completely different in tone and approach: Scene 1: *All Messages Deleted* is a series of messages left on Anne's telephone answering machine; Scene 6: *Mum and Dad* seems to be an interview of some kind with Anne's parents, and gives the impression that Anne may have committed a terrorist act, and may have killed herself; Scene 7: *The New Anny* takes the form of a commercial for a new car (or vehicle), the 'Anny'. There is no causal link between any of these scenes or within the scenes as they develop, yet I would definitely say that the action of the play moves forward scene by scene. It does so by means of accumulation, juxtaposition and contrast, which can also be regarded as forms of action and reaction.

By the end of Crimp's play, we have a very strong sense of Anne; and yet it is difficult to say with any degree of certainty exactly what that sense consists of. I will discuss the particular structural method Crimp uses (juxtaposition) in Chapter 6, but for now, consider what is the change the action of the play has brought about (the overriding purpose of the action). In Chapter 3, I talked about lateral movement, from ignorance to knowledge; here, Crimp effects that change solely in the audience, moving us from ignorance of Anne and what she represents to a kind of uneasy knowledge – uneasy, because we can't pin it down securely. It is a play with the same kind of disturbing, elusive energy as *The Servant*, though achieved in a very different way.

CHARACTER PURPOSE V. PURPOSE OF THE DRAMATIC ACTION

Similarly, we can identify a distinction between the purpose of the overall action of the play (the dramatic action) and the individual purpose of a character, arising from her own desire and will. The purpose of the overall action is to bring about change – in Todorov's pattern, to move from the opening balance to a new closing balance; it is not a psychological purpose, simply a logic of movement and momentum, like a stone rolling down a hill.

Each character in the play will, however, have a purpose that is particular to him, and this will be rooted in his psyche. He may or may not know at the outset of the play what is the nature of his own purpose (he may not, at the outset, appear to have one at all); his arc throughout the play could therefore be a voyage of self-discovery, as the play's action reveals to him what his true purpose is. Sometimes the two coincide: in this case, we think of the play as being 'character-driven'. We mean that what a character wants and sets out to get (the movement from lack to gain, perhaps), creates the action of the play: it is the change he wants that the action either delivers or refuses. However it's often the case that what the individual character wants may run counter to the logic of the dramatic action – that is, the action produces change that the character tries to resist.

The relationship between those two streams of purpose – that of the play's dramatic action and that of the individual character – is vital. It will define character, shape the unfolding of the action, and govern your storytelling

A View from the Bridge

In Arthur Miller's play, the central character Eddie Carbone obsessively idolizes his niece Catherine, who also has a deep reciprocal affection for him. He doesn't want anything to change that situation. When Catherine falls in love with an illegal immigrant and chooses him over Eddie, he takes drastic steps to prevent her leaving. The logical direction of the action – the replacement of her childhood attachment to Eddie by an adult partnership (that will also be a sexual one) – is fought by Eddie every step of the way. In the end, he is defeated, but in a manner that is much more disastrous than it would otherwise have been had he not resisted. Miller links the logic of the play's action to a human pattern whose inevitability we instantly recognize: the twin processes of growing up and the concomitant parental loss that that entails. Eddie's resistance is thus futile and obstinate, but it is profoundly understandable.

choices. It will play a central role in revealing what is the story you're telling your audience. Think, for example, about the difference between *The Servant* and *Oedipus the King*, as we discussed them in Chapter 3. Barrett has a very clearly distinguishable purpose – he wants to dominate Tony completely. We don't know why he wants that, but we are in no doubt that he does want it. Everything he does contrives to advance his purpose. The logic of the play's overall action matches it: each step Barrett takes inevitably increases Tony's dependence upon him. Notice that it is inevitable because of the nature of Tony's personality – without this match between Barrett's underlying drive and Tony's pliability, the play's overall action would be different: it would be an even-handed battle between them, or would be a very short play indeed if Tony pulled rank and sacked Barrett once and for all. It would not be – as it in fact is – a play in which a weak young man colludes in his own destruction. This is a nice example of a play in which a character's purpose drives the play's action.

Oedipus the King, on the other hand, is an example of the play's action running counter to the character's purpose – and where the two are in opposition, it is the character's purpose that must eventually give way. In *Oedipus*, we begin with a very strong character purpose: the King's desire for knowledge to solve Thebes' problem. His rejection of Teiresias' warning is our first indication of a deviation between the action of the play and Oedipus' individual purpose. He ignores the warning and demands an answer; at that point, he begins to run counter to the direction of the play's action. The overall purpose of the play's action is to reveal his identity and to complete the working out of his destiny – and Oedipus runs smack into it, as if he were running into a wall. From the moment Teiresias replies, Oedipus is scrambling to assimilate the staggering information and to get back on course with his own individual purpose. The action of the play is relentless, however, and offers him a stark choice: either abandon his purpose, save himself and let Thebes starve, or achieve his purpose, save Thebes and pay the personal price. *Oedipus the King* is an example of a play where the action gradually drives the character.

In the best plays, the relationship between the two constantly shifts back and forth – a kind of status reversal between them – so that character and action drive each other at different moments. To help you work through that shifting relationship, two key aspects of the structure of dramatic action can be used:

- Motivation
- The inciting incident

MOTIVATION – THE IMPORTANCE OF THE QUESTION WHY?

Of the six questions – where? when? who? why? what? how? – the most insistent one for contemporary audiences seems to be why? We want to identify causes, to understand reasons: we want explanations because we believe this will give us control of situations through an ability to predict their occurrence, control of our lives and our circumstances. This is wonderful for a playwright: you can, if you wish, structure your play by setting up a problem of some kind and then proceed to explore, explain and solve it. It's a clear, neat pattern that the audience will lock onto very quickly, and it answers a very strong desire in them.

But it's also quite dangerous for a playwright and potentially restrictive. The most absorbing plays are often those that don't answer questions neatly, but instead throw up more questions, taking us deeper and deeper into the complexities of human behaviour. Simple answers to why? often tend to be rather superficial ones, usually too pat to be adequately true; and sometimes the most disturbing truth is that there is no available satisfactory answer. It is, for example, the maiuetic nature of why? (the open-ended question) that underpins our fascination with the character of Iago and his destruction of the Moor in Shakespeare's *Othello*. Iago has been described, most effectively, as 'motiveless malignity' – a character without an identifiable set of reasons for his behaviour.

Nonetheless, what prompts us constantly to re-engage with Iago is the strength of our belief that *somewhere* there are reasons, and so we ask the question why? again and again, sifting the sequences of action to uncover them. As with the Prisoner's Dilemma scenario in Chapter 2, we move through a series of different positions and perspectives to try to find a satisfactory solution. We believe, at base, that Iago is acting out of his own desire and will, rather than randomly; we believe in the presence of an underlying, albeit concealed, *motivation*. Think of this term as the engine that drives action to produce movement. It is also the term that underpins much Western actor training, and will therefore be likely to form the basis of your actors' working approach to your characters.

DESIRE, NEED, FEAR AND WILL

The Russian director Stanislavsky suggested the actor should ask at each stage of the action 'What does my character want?' The actor should assume that the character has a goal, and is always working towards it; the goal is the fulfilment of a particular desire, and thus every act is a willed one (whether consciously acknowledged as such or not). Stanislavsky termed this the character's own 'through-line of action'. It's also a very useful place for you to begin. But there is one element that Stanislavsky didn't point to, in highlighting the role of desire, and that is the existence of need.

It is worth thinking about 'What does the character need?' alongside 'What does the character want?', because sometimes the two run in parallel (and thus desire is both justified and amplified by need) and sometimes they run counter to each other (and thus pull in different directions).

There are many levels of need: physical, emotional, intellectual. Some are practical issues – the need for sufficient means to purchase the necessities of life, for example. Others are more complex; the need for

affection, or for a feeling of security. Need amplifies desire when it crosses over from simple pragmatism to the emotional level. Think of a person whose ambition (the desire for success) is rooted in a deep need to be publicly acknowledged and approved – we describe their desire as 'burning', 'driving', even 'obsessive'.

But also think of the difference between what an addictive personality needs and what he *wants*: what he wants is what he's addicted to – alcohol, junk food, gambling. What he *needs* is not to have them, because having them only fuels his addiction further; however, he deludes himself that he 'needs' them, simply because he wants them – the delusion is a function of his addiction. In fact, desire and need are in opposition, in a tug-of-war for control of the character's actions.

The third component is fear, which occupies a pivotal role between the other two. Sometimes, what we want is the exact opposite of what we most fear: the desire to extend life as long as possible is prompted by the fear of death, for example. At other times, desire and fear coincide: think of the fears that often beset the bride and groom on their wedding day! Wanting to become one half of a bound-together couple can't disguise the trepidation accompanying the loss of the (familiar) single state. In the case of need, ambition that is obsessive entails a terror of failure. The addictive personality, confusing desire and his real needs, deep down, knows that he is deceiving himself; he is afraid of the truth.

The relationship between need, desire and fear is an important one. It is also one of which the character may be unaware (or may be unaware of the true nature of the relationship) at the start of the play. So the arc of the play's overall action may actually be the revelation to the character of the true relationship between the three – the self-revelation we explored earlier.

MAPPING PSYCHOLOGICAL DRIVES

Mapping the character's psychological drives helps you to establish the pitch of her personal stakes. Thinking about desire, need and fear also helps you to identify basic instinctual drives: food, shelter, sex, self-preservation, for example. Freud also included, in this group, what he called 'the territorial imperative' (the drive to occupy land or personal space). These basic drives are widely regarded as the most powerful of all.

Mapping and calibrating the drives on an ascending scale of 1-10 also helps you work out what exactly will be the incremental actions the character takes in order to achieve her goal: if, for example, her desire is a 10, she is likely to take a more extreme course of action, and be more determined, less likely to be deflected, than if her desire is only a 3.

GAGARIN WAY (2001)

In *Gagarin Way*, by Gregory Burke, the setting is Scotland, a factory in a depressed urban

---

Checklist: Desire, Fear and Need

- What does the character most desire? Be specific and precise.
- How badly does she want this? (On a scale of 1–10, in which 1 is low and 10 high, what number would you give to the intensity?)
- Does she actually need the thing she wants, or is it solely a desire?
- If she needs it, does the desire outweigh the need – would she still want it even if she didn't need it? (Give the degrees of desire and need numbers on a scale of 1–10; if need outweighs desire, need might be 9, but desire only 4, for example; if desire outweighs need, the numbers might be reversed. Be precise in your choice of numbers)
- If she would still want it anyway, why is this so?
- What are the limits she will go to in order to get what she wants?
- Why are these her limits? (Does she have strong morals? Would it involve harming someone else for whom she cares more? Is she afraid of the consequences?)

Then identify her fears:

- What does she most strongly *not* want? (Express it like this, rather than 'What does she least desire? Go for strength rather than weakness, it helps to provoke action)
- How badly does she not want it? (Number on the 1–10 scale?)
- Does she need to avoid it, or is it solely a desire to do so?
- Which is stronger here – need or desire? (Number on the scale, again)
- Why does she not want it/fear it?
- What are the limits she'll go to in order to avoid it?
- Why are these her limits?

Attaching numbers to the intensity encourages precision and acts as a quick reminder as you develop the character's behaviour whether or not you've pitched it correctly.

area. A security guard, Tom (a young university graduate who is, he hopes, only marking time until he gets what he considers to be a proper job), is on night shift. As the play opens, Tom is sitting in a storeroom talking to Eddie, an older factory worker. We learn quite quickly that Tom believes he is turning a blind eye (for a small bribe) to a bit of pilfering of computer chips by Eddie and his partner in crime, Gary, whose arrival they are both awaiting. It soon emerges that Eddie has duped Tom, and he and Gary are in fact engaged in something very much worse involving kidnapping and intended murder.

For Tom, the stakes are actually not terribly high at the outset. What he says he wants is a 'proper job', and this isn't it. But he doesn't appear to be aggressively seeking to improve the situation (although he does claim to have a number of job applications in circulation), so obviously he doesn't want it very badly. Maybe a 3 on the scale, perhaps. And as he has a job and a wage in an economically depressed area, he doesn't appear desperately to need to improve the situation, either – probably only a 2 on the scale. He wants a proper job really because he's young and he's bored. In the short term, he wants some excitement, a bit of interest to pass the long night shift, and so he agrees to Eddie's bribe. You could explore that short-term desire also in terms of numbers. How badly does he want the excitement? Is it a need or just a desire? Is his desire for excitement greater than his desire for a proper job?

Certainly, it's greater in the short term, so this gives us another element in thinking about desire and need: time. How badly does the character want something, and how urgently? ('I want it and I want it *now*.') Does the urgency ratchet up the intensity? In a lot of instances, the answer is yes it does, and it is this which tends to make a character very vulnerable. (Time helps you to create compression and intensification.) It is so in Tom's case, as we can see if we look at what might be his fears.

At university, Tom studied politics, economics and philosophy ('a tiny little bit'). He has thus explored (at the theoretical level) concepts of right and wrong, and has also examined such concepts ambiguously in practice in political dealings. He is quite a naive young man but he is not vicious, as we see once it becomes clear to him what Eddie's and Gary's true purpose is. He really doesn't want to be involved in killing. He knew that Eddie's pilfering was wrong, but that didn't stop him accepting the bribe; this, however, is a very different matter, and so his desire for this not to involve him would attract a higher number on our 1–10 scale. Perhaps a 7. It's becoming clearer to us what Tom's limits are, and why those are his limits.

There is, however, a greater problem still for Tom, once Gary arrives with the kidnap victim. The original plan was for him simply to open the gate for Gary, and to remain there on duty, but he doesn't: he comes back to collect his uniform cap that he had forgotten, and so he sees what Gary has brought. At first Tom is confused (not aided by the fact that Gary immediately hits him with a cosh), but then Eddie tells him what he and Gary intend to do. This raises the stakes for Tom. He's now not only involved in kidnapping and intended murder, but Eddie and Gary refuse to let him leave. If he tries to leave, they'll kill him; they won't accept his promise not to tell the police.

The stakes are sky-high now. Outweighing Tom's desire not to be involved in kidnap and murder is now a clear 10: the desire not to die himself. We can tell that this one outweighs the other desire because eventually he stays (and thus risks becoming an accessory to the crimes). Again, his limits are clear, and they make sense – self-preservation is one of the strongest of all drives: it is more than a desire, it is an instinctual need. From this point on, Tom's actions are governed by the interplay between the two: self-preservation, and the fear of being involved in a capital crime. But they have arisen because of what he wanted at the outset of the play – a bit of excitement – which, in turn, arose because his desire for a 'proper job' was insufficiently strong to motivate him. If it had been stronger, he probably wouldn't still have been working at the factory.

Like Tom, Eddie and Gary have their own desires, needs and fears that give them their motivation. For them, both older than Tom, the situation is different. They don't have Tom's educational advantages, and lack his potential for improving his employment status. They lack Tom's possible future; theirs is blighted, as it is likely that the factory will be adversely affected by recent changes in ownership. For them, their action in kidnapping and intending to kill Frank, the company's representative, is an avowed political gesture: the individual's retaliation against the dehumanization of global free market capitalism, as they see it.

Tom's unexpected reappearance creates a disruption in the forward momentum of their intended project. A second, greater disruption is caused by Gary's insistence on talking to Frank before they kill him. That decision, together with the presence of the reluctant Tom, changes everything and eventually uncovers a much more chilling motivation in Eddie: he is actually a psychopath.

The interaction of desire, need, fear and will within each of the characters (Tom, Eddie, Gary and Frank), and between the characters motivates the play's overall action. It is the collision between the different strands that provokes decisions of an increasingly dark nature; decisions that lead to catastrophic behaviours. But it is these collisions, decisions and behaviours that ultimately uncover the most chilling truth – Eddie's true nature. Perhaps we could say, therefore, that the overall purpose of the play's action was this revelation: as in *Oedipus the King*, the arc of dramatic action is the revelation of who (or what) someone really is. However, whereas in *Oedipus* the revelation is given to the character as well as to the audience, in *Gagarin Way* the revelation is given only to us: Eddie does not discover anything about himself. He already knows.

SCRIPT EXERCISE: PART A

The next writing exercise is in three parts, building a longer scene out of the two elements of action under discussion in this chapter. You could choose to do each element separately, after each discussion, or if you prefer, you could wait until the end of the chapter and then do all three exercises together. Whichever you choose to do, keep the exercises together, because the characters we're exploring now build into the eventual scene.

Study the two young women in Fig. 8, Characters D and E.

- They are smiling. Do they know each other? Are they perhaps friends?
- They seem to be in the middle of some kind of exchange. What do you think is going on between them?
- There are hints of other people being present, and a string of balloons in the background. They are at a party. What might the party be for?
- Where do you think they are?
- When is this taking place? (Their clothing might suggest the season, and the lights in the background might suggest time of day)

Write a character profile for D and for E.

Figure 8   Characters D and E.

- Start with the obvious information in the picture: age, sex, race, and so on (the kind of information we considered in our first thoughts about status in Chapter 3).
- Using the questions above, flesh out the skeleton of the situation: where they are, when it is, what's going on around them and between them.
- Build on those details: who are they? Give them names, a background, some kind of history.
- Delve into their 'inner lives', using our earlier questions about desire and need. Are there any hints in the picture that might help you? E has her hand resting on her throat: is she perhaps denying something? ('Who, me?' 'I certainly did not!') Has D challenged her in some way? D's eyes are closed: she's refusing eye contact with E. Is

she, perhaps, refusing to accept E's denial? Or is the boot on the other foot, and it's E who is insisting on something (the hand on the throat could be emphatic) and D who is being challenged? Both women are smiling: are the smiles genuine or are they fake?
- Try to focus your thoughts about desire and need specifically on this relationship between the two women: what do they want/need *from each other*? What do they not want (or need) from each other?

Fig. 8 builds into a sequence of four pictures that offer the stimulus for a scene. But it's not necessarily the first picture in the sequence. I'm using it here simply as a means of inviting you to think about two characters who will eventually become the two main characters in your scene.

65

If you choose to do the three exercises separately, don't worry if you find later that some of the ideas you have created here about D and E don't fit together with your ideas about the rest of the pictures. It could help you understand more about the relationship between character and situation, if that happens. The value of this exercise lies in thinking about character in terms of motivation: what drives him or her to take decisions and act upon them.

If the picture doesn't stimulate any ideas, you could seek out other pictures as the basis for your character profiles, or you could just use the lists of questions to imagine a pair of characters. In either case, try to construct a *pair* of characters, rather than two unrelated ones. The situation, however, should be the same: some kind of party.

As this is a cumulative exercise, some comments are offered at the end of Part C.

THE INCITING INCIDENT – WHERE DOES IT ALL BEGIN?

We've observed that action is a process that generates movement whose purpose is to produce change; and that the interplay between the character's needs, desires, fears and will is an excellent means of motivating action. But these psychological drives are often ongoing states within a character and thus are likely to exist long before the action of the play begins. So what makes it begin? Where does the play's action actually start?

The transformational arc requires a condition of balance at the outset of the story. You could think about this as a balance between the character and his context (between character and his surrounding world) and internally, within the character's needs, desires, and fears. This might be an ideal state, where the character is fully at ease with himself, his circumstances and his environ-

ment and is perfectly happy. But it need not be. Balance, as we are using the term, simply means a condition in which contrary forces that might create movement are evenly weighted. It is a condition of suspended movement. We might describe it as a state in which the possibly contrary pull of desire, fear and need have reached some kind of mutual accommodation (whether happy or unhappy), or where they have accommodated themselves in relation to the context. Tom, in *Gagarin Way*, has, at the outset of the play, just such an internal and external accommodation. It's not great, it's not what he would really like, but for now, he's living with it. Perhaps that's a useful way of thinking about the opening balance: it's what the characters are living with, for the moment.

The second step is disruption of the opening balance. This is where the action of the play begins, with 'the inciting incident'. In terms of the six basic questions, the inciting incident responds to 'what?': that is, what happens? Sometimes you might hear it referred to as the 'initiating' incident, pointing to its function, which is to begin the action. But 'inciting' is a stronger reminder of the link between what? and why? (the question of motivation): to incite is to call into action, to stir up, to set in motion, and again reiterates the importance of human agency.

The inciting incident is any occurrence that ruptures the previous state of accommodation and lifts the suspension of movement. Remember I used the term 'falling' earlier? The inciting incident is the off-balancing push. It is the inaugural element of the process of action, the trigger; without it, there can be no story, for nothing need be done. Something happens – it need not be large, it can be very tiny, apparently insignificant – but it must be enough to ruin the accommodation, and therefore initiate change. So, in thinking about the inciting incident, you need to ask 'what would make this condition of balance unsustainable?' And of course there will potentially be a considerable number of things that could do that.

PLANNING THE STORY DEVELOPMENT

This is where it's really valuable to spend substantial time planning the complete arc of your story from beginning to end, before you actually start to write scenes. (Though if you find it more conducive to write an unstructured rough draft and then pull it completely apart, do that. Planning focuses your thinking, but it doesn't necessarily fire up every writer's creative engine. Some writers say they need to write a draft before they find out what their story really is. But whether you expend energy first on a rough draft or not, you will need to do this structural work to achieve a lean and effective story. However uphill the task may seem, don't deceive yourself that you can avoid it and simply tinker with surface detail – you'll end up with something flabby, unconvincing and meandering!)

Perhaps you'll find it surprising – even disappointing – that you need to determine, from the outset, how your story will resolve (or to put it another way which suggests less of a pat ending, what will be the closing balance.) But it's important if you are going to create a story taut enough to keep the audience on the hook throughout. Remember that they are constantly looking to predict what is coming next, and although you will be trying sometimes to surprise them, you will also be rewarding them for guessing correctly at other times. You should avoid consistently or cumulatively frustrating and disappointing them (although, used very sparingly, frustration can be a provocative tool.) So, if you don't really know what happens next, how will they?

Five Stages of Story Development

The inciting incident isn't a one-off occurrence: it's the first link in the causal chain, producing a reciprocal effect that, in turn becomes a new cause for a subsequent effect. It matches action with reaction. This sequential pattern helps you map five vital stages of the story development:

- inciting incident (the catalyst that kicks everything off-balance)
- complication (how the problem escalates)
- crisis (where the escalation reaches its worst point)
- climax (where the peak of escalation decisively reverses)
- resolution (how the recovery is completed).

Think of it in terms of a journey: how often do you embark on one without knowing where you're trying to get to? Planning the arc of your story from inciting incident to resolution is like planning a route map; it allows you to take enjoyable little side-trips without losing your way.

PAST, PRESENT AND FUTURE

The six basic questions frequently allude to three tenses, or aspects of time: past, present and future. In asking why something is happening, you'll often reach into the past to search for the reasons. Setting your characters' goals in the present also motivates their future. So there is an element of when? always at work.

In the case of what?, all three tenses come into play:

- what has happened before
- what is happening now
- what will happen next

Past, present and future help you to map the complete arc of action. Notice that, in terms of cause and effect, the events of the past may become the cause of the events of the present (the effect); these present events, in turn, will become the cause of the events in the future (effects).

THE IMAGE/SHADOW METHOD

In your story planning, the opening balance (which responds to the basic question where?) reflects what has happened before. We may not need to be told about the specifics of those occurrences – that will depend upon the story you're telling. But whether we do or don't need to know the specifics, what we're seeing at the outset of the play are the effects of the past embodied in the present moment. For example, if we see an ordered, peaceful, prosperous world in the opening balance, we understand that it is so because of previous actions to establish order, create wealth and resolve conflict. But the seeds of the future are also embodied in the present, in the potential for change: if order is not maintained, chaos will ensue; if the conditions for wealth disappear, it will be replaced by poverty; peace is fragile, war never far away.

Therefore, as you make preliminary notes on the opening condition of balance in your story, make a parallel set that details the mirror opposite (its 'shadow', a term I've borrowed from Christopher Vogler's *The Writer's Journey: Mythic Structure for Storytellers and Screenwriters*). It can sometimes be useful to create the two sets simultaneously, on adjacent pages of your notebook. Match detail for detail: if the world is a prosperous one in the opening balance, match it with an impoverished one in its shadow version; if it is a cruel and unjust place at first, its shadow will be compassionate and fair. By doing this, you can begin to map the past and future: the shadow is what it once was, or could become. It is memory, or prophecy, and points to what the closing balance, or elements of it, may be. If you wanted to think spatially, as we have done before, you could perhaps consider the relationship between past, present and future in terms of background and foreground.

Creating both the image and shadow versions of the opening balance allows scope for layering the three tenses simultaneously into each other, so that even as we are looking at what is happening now, we can see traces of what has gone before, and hints of what is to come. Layering gives depth, subtlety and

'Enough to Ruin the Accommodation'

It's important to avoid setting the pitch of the action too high too soon, for you need scope to raise the stakes and build narrative tension as the story develops into complication. This is the 'rising arc', moving upwards towards first, the crisis point and then, the climax. Once you have some notes on the overall metamorphosis, go back and ask, of each detail: 'what is the least it would take to turn x detail into its shadow?' The inciting incident need only be enough to ruin the accommodation. The detail-by-detail examination can help keep the pitch of the inciting incident at the minimum necessary level. Find where the balance is most precariously located, and apply just enough pressure to tip it over and begin the chain-reaction.

texture to the opening balance. But the image/shadow versions also help you to identify what the inciting incident has to be. In looking from one to the other, ask 'what would need to happen to turn the opening balance into its shadow form?'

'HERE' AND 'NOW' V. 'THERE' AND 'THEN'

Sometimes, in analysing play structure, the inciting incident can be confused with the opening balance, particularly in cases where the balance is less than ideal. In *Oedipus the King*, we noted that the opening balance is a terrible state of affairs: Thebes blighted by famine and drought, its people suffering. It is a condition ripe for change; clearly, change, in the form of improvement, is desperately needed. We might feel that this terrible condition is itself an incitement to action, and indeed it is. But it is not, in dramatic terms, the inciting incident; it is the existing condition at the outset of the play. The inciting incident, the 'something that happens', has yet to occur.

A useful way of thinking about the difference between the opening balance and the inciting incident is, once again, via time and space. The opening balance is a condition that has already begun *before* your play begins; it is the last few moments of 'then'. In spatial terms, it is offstage ('there'). What we see, therefore, as your play opens, are the signs of 'there' and 'then'. The inciting incident is onstage ('here'); in terms of time, it marks the decisive moment at which 'then' ceases, and the present moment (the 'now') of the action commences. It is rather important that the inciting incident should happen onstage rather than offstage, in the present moment rather than in the past. But there are a number of inventive ways in which events can be brought onstage, into the present moment.

THE BEAUTY QUEEN OF LEENANE (1996)

Let's explore the kinds of things that can serve as inciting incidents, and the possible value of using offstage/onstage (there/here) and then/now as ways of thinking.

In Martin McDonagh's *The Beauty Queen of Leenane*, Maureen Folan is a 40-year-old spinster trapped in a relationship of spiteful mutual dependency with her 70-year-old mother, Mag. The play opens in 'The living room/kitchen of a rural cottage in the west of Ireland', as Maureen returns from shopping. McDonagh quickly establishes the opening balance for us, signalling the routine nature of the two women's lives and their petty frictions. They bicker about the preparation of Mag's Complan drink, Mag whines about her porridge, Maureen detects a suspicious whiff from the sink that betrays Mag's habitual crime of emptying her chamber pot there. We recognize immediately that these are habits and routines that have existed long before the play begins, and will continue unless something intervenes to change them.

As he establishes these patterns of behaviour, McDonagh also gives us hints as to the motivation for change. Maureen hates this pattern of life ('just a blessed fecking skivvy is all I'm thought of!'), and focuses her resentment on what she sees as its cause: Mag ('...that sounds the type of fella I would like to meet, and then bring him home to meet you, if he likes murdering oul women.') For Maureen, the opening balance is a condition of imprisonment; she is longing for escape. If we were to detail the image/shadow versions of the opening balance, we would note that there are two possible shadow versions of the detail 'Maureen lives with her mother': 'Maureen lives with somebody else' and 'Maureen lives alone'.

In terms of Maureen's desire, it is very much the first of those two alternatives she would like, and she would most particularly like the 'somebody else' to be a man – a sexual partner, a husband. But if she is to pursue this goal, two aspects of her circumstances must alter: Mag must go, and a man must arrive. In her very tightly circumscribed world, how is this to happen? Mag will only go if she is put into a nursing home or if she dies. But going into a home is what Mag fears, and so she will resist Maureen every step of the way. On this front, they are deadlocked. As far as death is concerned, though Mag is elderly and a bit rickety, she is robust enough to frustrate Maureen's hopes there, too ('I suppose now you'll never be dying. You'll be hanging on forever, just to spite me.') So Maureen is stuck with Mag. This is the opening balance in its truest form: Maureen constantly but impotently wanting her mother to be gone, so that she might be free to live with the desired man (whoever he might be.)

In the small village, there is a dearth of available men who could free Maureen by marrying her – and she is reaching middle age, so her opportunities seem to be narrowing even faster. Many of the village men have already left to seek work else-where, in England or America: one of those men is Pato Dooley, a man Maureen has known for many years. Pato's been working in England but has returned briefly to Leenane for a family celebration, a party for his American relatives who are about to go home to Boston; he will shortly depart, too, back to England.

PATO DOOLEY: THE DETAIL THAT RUINS THE ACCOMMODATION

Pato's presence is the detail that is capable of ruining the (unhappy) accommodation Maureen has reached with her situation, the detail that is capable of transforming the image version of the opening balance into its shadow form. But there were two versions of the shadow; in one, Maureen would go off with Pato Dooley, in the other Maureen would be left alone without him. The arc of the play's action is the movement towards one or other of these two possible outcomes. But which will it be? McDonagh works a series of accumulating reversals, in which the characters move back and forth between the two possibilities, until the final sequence. This sequence is a series of revelations, beginning with Maureen's discovery that, thanks to Mag's treachery, she has lost the chance of the outcome she desired. The final moments reveal what she does to turn the opening balance detail ('Maureen lives with her mother') decisively into its shadow form.

If Pato Dooley is the detail that is capable of upsetting the opening balance, then the inciting incident has to be something to do with Pato. We could point to the fact of his brief return from England as an 'incitement', but this is where the onstage ('here'/ 'now') aspect of the inciting incident is really crucial. For Pato has already returned from England when the play opens; so his return is part of the pre-existing condition at the outset – that is, although it is very recent, it occurred offstage ('there'/ 'then'.) And it has not yet upset the opening balance between Maureen and Mag.

Consider: from the information above, what needs to happen now in order for the opening balance to be upset?

Clearly, in order for the accommodation Maureen has made with her daily life to be ruined, she has to meet Pato again, and in a new light, so that the chain of causes and effects that will lead to her departure with him can begin. The most obvious choice would be for Maureen and Pato to meet onstage, in front of us. Perhaps he could come to visit her (but this would have to be plausibly motivated), or Maureen could go to meet Pato, and the location could shift to wherever they meet, in order for us to see them meet. But if the location shifts, McDonagh would lose the oppressive power of the constant physical setting ('The living room/ kitchen of a rural cottage in the west of Ireland'); it's important for our emotional understanding of Maureen's condition that the stage space doesn't change so early in the play. It would release quite a lot of the pressure upon her.

KEEPING THE FOCUS

There's a further problem: if the onstage action shows us Maureen meeting Pato again, there is a possible risk that we will – however briefly – lose sight of the central arc of action that tracks the relationship between Maureen and Mag. It is not, after all, a play about Maureen and Pato. This is important: losing the focus from Maureen and Mag would be another form of spatial displacement from onstage to offstage and would thus dissipate the energy generated by compressing the action between the mother/ daughter pair. So the Maureen-Pato meeting has to occur, but cannot become the 'main event'; it must be the occasion of another skirmish between Maureen and Mag, so that the focus is kept on them. The meeting probably needs to occur offstage, so that the skirmish it causes can occur onstage.

And this is what McDonagh does. In Scene Two, while Maureen is out feeding the chickens, a new character arrives: Ray Dooley, Pato's brother, who still lives at home in Leenane. He has a message for Maureen: an invitation to the 'going-away do' for the Dooleys' American relatives – which is why Pato has come home to Leenane from England.

But Maureen is out, so he writes down the message on a bit of paper, and leaves it with Mag to give to Maureen, which she promises faithfully to do. Except, of course, she doesn't, at all.

    As Ray's footsteps fade, Mag gets
    up, reads the message on the table,
    goes to the kitchen window and
    glances out, then finds a box of
    matches, comes back to the table,
    strikes a match, lights the message,
    goes to the range with it burning
    and drops it inside. Sound of
    footsteps approaching the front
    door. Mag shuffles back to her
    rocking chair and sits in it just as
    Maureen enters.

This is a lovely example of how to construct an inciting incident. The invitation brought by Ray is, quite literally, a 'call to action', and if successful, will bring about the required meeting between Pato and Maureen. But that is still in the future, at this point. The focus is on Mag and Maureen. Since Maureen is not in to receive the 'call' herself, it falls to Mag to receive it on her behalf. It is what Mag does that is crucial in determining the outcome of the play.

Inevitability

The inciting incident should be the thing that will make the eventual resolution inevitable. That's why it's so important to work out, at the outset, not only how your play begins but also how it ends, because the one determines the other, gives it proper shape. It is this sense of shape that the audience latches onto and begins to predict what will happen – a process in which, you will remember, you want them to engage.

71

A SMALL-SCALE INCIDENT

The inciting incident here is the issuing of an invitation to attend the party (at which Maureen will meet Pato again). It is issued onstage by Ray on behalf of the Dooley family, and actually includes Mag as well as Maureen. This is super writing; giving this vital action to a minor character helps to keep the scale of the inciting incident quite small. If Pato came onstage to deliver the invitation himself, then this could be too big an event at such an early point in the action – it could displace the focus from Mag and Maureen to Maureen and Pato. It would undermine McDonagh's ability to raise the dramatic stakes by bringing him onstage later, once his relationship with Maureen has begun (which he does in Scene Three).

It is also a nice touch that the invitation is extended to both women, not just to Maureen. It makes Mag's decision to destroy the note all the more perverse; she is not acting out of a wounded sense of exclusion, but out of pure spite. Once again, McDonagh keeps the action onstage between Mag and Maureen, rather than allowing it to be displaced offstage into an opposition between Mag and the Dooleys.

THE CHAIN OF ACTION

In *Beauty Queen*, the inciting incident is the moment at which Maureen and Mag are set onto an irrevocable collision course. It seems to revolve around Pato Dooley, but is really a collision between the two women's conflicting desires, fears, needs and wills.

But the inciting incident is a beginning, not an ending – it opens a door rather than closes it – so the incident and the reactive decision that accompanies it must be followed by something that allows the chain of action to continue and build. So, of course, Maureen must find out about the invitation in time to go to the party; she does, by the simple expedient of bumping into Ray (offstage) as she returns from feeding the chickens. He tells her about leaving the invitation note with Mag, and thus sets up the ensuing onstage action: Maureen's revelation of Mag's treachery.

This skirmish Maureen wins, and she punishes Mag by inflicting upon her a horribly lumpy drink of badly mixed Complan. This is 'what happens now'. But there are two other tenses to be considered in answer to 'what'?

- What has happened before? (past)
- What will happen next? (future)

The Importance of Characters' Decisions

The decision that a character takes as an immediate result of the inciting incident occurring, triggers the disruption of balance and starts the movement of the dramatic action. This is the crux of rooting the action of your play in character rather than in events. Dramatic action is really about what people do. The inciting incident itself may be something that is done by a person or it may be an external occurrence (the appearance of a ghost, a storm), but if you pay attention to the verb (to incite), you'll see that you are trying to pinpoint exactly what it is that will motivate a character to *do* something. The inciting incident must always provoke a decision that gives rise to an act. The decision and the act may be willed, or may be instinctive reflex, but the motivation will reside in the tension between desire, fear and need.

The pattern of betrayal, discovery and revenge we see here is also the pattern of past and future action. It points forward, as a kind of prophecy, to what will happen later: a second invitation that Mag again receives (via Ray) and that she again withholds from Maureen. This time however Mag appears to win the skirmish, for Maureen doesn't find out about the invitation in time to take it up. But the rising arc of action dictates that this second invitation will be a greater one than the first, and it is: it's an invitation from Pato to Maureen to go away with him – what she has most wanted, but that Mag has most feared. Through Mag's treachery, Maureen loses her one chance of escape into the ideal shadow version of the opening balance detail (Maureen lives with Pato Dooley). So there is then only one alternative shadow version left: Maureen lives alone. For that to occur, Mag has to go, into a nursing home or a coffin.

The pattern of action established by the inciting incident is one of betrayal/ discovery/revenge, and so we expect that pattern to be replayed again. Because of the rising arc, the repeat of the pattern will this time have to be greater. But it does not come out of a clear blue sky. It has been foreshadowed in the 'there' and 'then' elements of the opening balance. McDonagh gives us a tiny clue in the opening stage direction, in his description of Mag: 'Her left hand is somewhat more shrivelled and red than her right.'

In retaliation for Mag's treachery over the second invitation letter, Maureen puts onto the range a pan of cooking oil, heats it, holds down Mag's shrivelled left hand and cold-bloodedly pours the boiling oil over it. The act is vicious, and we recognize with a shock that this is not a new occurrence: Mag's red and shrivelled hand at the start of the play is the effect of a long process of brutality by Maureen. What we see her do here, she has done before.

The rising arc tells us that what she will do next, in the climax of the play, will be worse still. It is, and it brings about the resolution (the closing balance), by turning the opening balance detail (Maureen lives with Mag) into its only remaining shadow version (Maureen lives alone): a resolution to which McDonagh gives a particularly gothic twist in order to deliver a mirror image of the opening of the play. It's a distinctly creepy final image, but very satisfying in its logic: the movement of the overall action comes to rest at the point we have, in truth, known all along it must reach.

SCRIPT EXERCISE: PART B

In Part A, you created two young women characters, and sketched the skeleton of a party situation, from the stimulus of Figure 8. (Or you perhaps chose your own picture, or just used the questions.) So you have some notes on 'who?', 'where?', 'when?' and the beginnings of 'what?' and 'why?'. Part B fleshes out the arc of a story sequence involving these two women: to develop 'what?' and begin to think about 'how?' – not just what happens, but how you tell the story. Here, you plan the outline of your story that will finally become a fully scripted sequence in Part C.

Look at the four pictures: Figures 9, 10, 11 and 12:

- Fig. 9 shows more of the party situation. Notice that the two women are not present in this picture.
- Our former Fig. 8 (your two characters) now becomes Fig. 10 in the sequence.
- Fig. 11 shows a group of people at the party looking at a photograph album.
- Fig. 12 gives you a different perspective of the group. Notice that from this point of view, your two characters are included.

Figure 9   The opening balance.

Figure 10   The central characters.

Figure 11   A source of information.

Figure 12   Proximity.

- Fig. 9 is your opening balance. Write a couple of paragraphs describing this story world: where, when, who, and what is the occasion. In your description, be as economical as possible, but try to use rich, evocative language. Focus on just a few key details. Think about things we see or hear that will tell us immediately what we need to know.
- In note form, plan how you will introduce your two central characters (Fig. 10). How do we first encounter them? What are they doing? How do we find out who they are?

Now you have your opening balance, and your two central characters established within it. But as yet, there is no story.

- Look at your character profile notes about the women, in particular, at your notes about the relationship between them, and about desire and need. What did you decide that D wanted and/or needed from E? What didn't D want/need? What did E want/ need/ not want/ not need from D?
- Identify something they both want, or that they both fear (don't want). What is it? (An object? A piece of information? A feeling?)
- Go back to the opening balance. The first indication of the object of the women's desires or fears should appear here. Find where it is. (It might be an object, or a hint as to the information. If it's to do with feelings or relationships, there should be a hint as to the people concerned.)
- Only one of the two women, in this story, can have what she wants, or avoid what she fears. The other one loses, and/or gets what she fears, if the lucky one is successful. So the two women are on a collision course. What will the unlucky one get?

This gives you the arc of the story: both women want something and set out to get it.

- Who gets it, by the end of the story?
- What happens to the relationship between them, as a result?

This gives you the resolution, and a key element of the closing balance.

- How do the women first become aware of the existence (or location) of the desired/ feared object/information/feeling at the party? What is the first thing to happen that makes it possible for one of them to get it (or avoid it)?
- Do they both realize at the same time? Do they both realize that only one can have/avoid it? Do they realize at the same time, or at different times?

This gives you the inciting incident. Now develop the full arc of action:

- What does each woman do, in order to achieve her goal? Wherever possible, keep them on a collision course, so that each action by one woman makes it harder for the other to achieve success.
- What is the turning point, where the lucky one wins and the unlucky one loses?
- The resolution delivers the closing balance. It shows us the victor and the loser, and what is now the relationship between them. What elements of the opening balance have now changed? As with the opening balance, write a short paragraph describing it, in rich but economical language: key details, what we see and hear that tells us what we need to know. Where are the two characters now, in relation to each other?

You haven't been directed specifically to use Figs 11 and 12. That's deliberate. It's up to you whether or not you want to use the material in those pictures. In Chapter 3, in the exercise on revelation and discovery, mobile phones and pieces of paper offered means of transmitting information. Here, the photograph album in Fig. 11 is another potential means. Fig. 12 puts the two women in proximity to the album. If you find this promising for your story, use it. If not, feel free to ignore it, and develop the story however you wish.

If you've decided not to work from the pictures, you can use the two characters and the party situation you created in Part A as your opening balance. Follow the suggestions above to help you map out the course of the action.

Whether you work from the picture stimulus or not, you are working towards a story sequence about a pair of central characters that moves forward in identifiable steps. From your notes above, track the series of steps, and give each complete step forward a new paragraph of its own (even if it's only one line), so you can clearly see the sequence of action develop. You should end up with a couple of pages of story outline.

SCRIPT EXERCISE: PART C

You now have a pair of characters at a party, and an outline of the action that unfolds between them. You know what they both want, which motivates the action; how it begins, how and why it develops, and how it ends.

Keeping the character profiles and the story outline beside you, write the scene. Try to follow the shape of the scene as you have plotted it in the outline, and to flesh out the inner lives of the two characters as your profiles suggest; in particular, use the numbers you've given to the desire/ fear/ need to help you set the stakes precisely.

This scene will be longer than the ones in Chapter 3: allow yourself eight to ten pages. Try to write it as one continuously developing scene, rather than a series of very short scenes.

Ask someone to read the scene afterwards; you want to know whether the characters are believable, their behaviour logical, and whether the story is both plausible and clear. Ask the reader to describe what happens, and why; compare their brief description with your outline. Have they understood your characters' motivations? You could ask them to pinpoint what it was in the script that told them.

COMMENTS
Developing character profiles and story

The Value of Planning

Thinking about character helps you find nuances and subtleties for the dialogue and physical action. Working out the arc of action helps you keep driving the story forward, building tension and suspense for the audience. You can be economical and gripping in your writing, but being clear about the patterns of movement within the story also allows you to create little moments of rest, for evocation of character, atmosphere and the story world. There lies the density and richness of texture in your script; the sense, for the audience, that these are real things happening to real people. But without planning carefully, it's all too easy to indulge yourself in these moments, and wander from the thrust of the story; pace and energy slacken, and the audience may lose its interest in your characters and their goals.

outlines are detailed tasks, but the most taxing of the three exercises is Part C, because it requires considerable discipline to keep within the pathways you have already laid down. The more disciplined you can be, the better you are able to test the strength of the material in Parts A and B. Conversely, the stronger and more accurate your planning, the better your scripted scene should be.

Rewriting

It's acknowledged by writers and script editors that good plays are not written, they are rewritten; the true art of good writing lies in your readiness to identify weak points, and to understand what to do to correct the problem. Sometimes the alterations need only be minor; at other times, the draft will have to be shelved, and the scene begun again in light of what has been learned. Experienced writers are willing to do either, as necessary, but scrapping a whole scene draft can be rather demoralizing for a new writer. It feels as though the draft has been wasted, nothing achieved. Actually, the opposite is the case. No draft, however unsuccessful, is ever a waste.

Choosing Details That Can Be Enacted

Was it difficult to translate the descriptive paragraphs of the opening and closing balance (in Part B) into dramatic script? This goes to the heart of the difference between writing prose and writing drama.

Look back at the key details in your description: were they sufficiently evocative of the world of the play? Were they details that could be *enacted* – that is, were they things we could principally *see* or *hear* for ourselves?

Theatre addresses itself principally to the eye and the ear, but the other three senses can also be used very richly onstage: rough or smooth textures, solids versus fluids, for example, can appeal to our sense of touch. Japanese director Yukio Ninagawa, in a production of Shakespeare's *A Midsummer Night's Dream*, first introduced the Mechanicals (the troupe of working men rehearsing amateur dramatics for the Duke's wedding celebrations) through the audience's noses and taste buds: the scene began in darkness with someone frying noodles in a wok. The smell was wonderful, mouth-watering, and told us in one moment everything we needed to know about the world these men inhabited. American playwright Tina Howe wrote an entire play, *The Art of Dining*, around the preparation and eating of a meal!

The Characters' Inner Lives

Probably the most difficult aspect will have been creating the inner lives of the two

Address Our Five Senses

The metaphors you choose should be capable of physical embodiment, rather than simply being confined to language. In your opening balance, the key details collaborate to begin to deliver those metaphors; in your closing balance, the details work to resolve and complete them. Go for key details that can be made to address directly at least one of our five senses – sight, sound, touch, taste, smell. A detail's look and sound (that can also appeal to touch), or its smell (that can also make us taste it), harnesses the audience's sensory equipment as points of access to their imagination.

women, their desires, fears and needs; and particularly, working out how each woman's inner life intersected with the other's. This area will most likely have involved you in a lot of rethinking and rewriting. It always will, so don't be dismayed by this.

The best stories grow naturally out of characters' responses to given situations. But it's also important to recognize that characters are more than just 'plot functionaries', there solely to carry out actions. Those will address what they do, but not the question why? And if why? is not a motivating question, then who? is not fully in play, either. We need a sense of depth – of what has been wonderfully termed the character's 'hinterland' – in order to involve ourselves in who your characters really are. We tend to look to characters' motivations – to potential answers to why? – to point to what underpins their actions. We look for the clues that will give us revelations. Working on the characters' inner lives allows us to mine what lies beneath the surface.

TENSIONS BETWEEN CHARACTER AND STORY

A problem may have occurred when you felt that your characters wouldn't plausibly do what was necessary to move the story forward properly. Be careful not to force them into performing actions for the sake of the story ; audiences will reject the actions as being 'out of character'.

LENGTH

Did you find it hard to fill eight to ten pages, or conversely, hard to confine it to this length?

In recent years, the tendency for plays to last about two hours including a 15-minute interval has been shifting; shorter plays are on

---

Checklist: Character v. Story

If your character wouldn't believably do what your story needs, ask:

- In what circumstances would he perform the action the story requires of him now? (What would have to be happening in his head/heart/body?)
- Are these the circumstances he's in now? If not, can those circumstances plausibly be created now? (What would trigger those internal responses?)
- If those circumstances aren't in place, or can't be created, what are the current circumstances?
- How would he react to those? Why would he react this way?
- Find the difference between the way he would react, and the way you need him to react. Then either rework the character profile to deliver the unforced response, or reconsider the story action to produce the 'in character' response.

The story advances when a character is provoked into a decision and acts upon it.

- Examine the moments of decision.
- What alternative decisions might he have made? Why did he make *this* decision?
- Having made his decision, think through the alternative courses of action he might have taken as a result. Why did he take *this* course?

the upsurge, and a significant number are now ninety minutes or under, without any interval. The most important consideration for you is the scope of the idea that drives the play – how much time is needed to tell the story in appropriate depth and detail. You're looking to balance pace and narrative tension with moments of rest, time for the audience to assimilate information and to be ready and eager for more.

If you found it hard to fill the pages, perhaps you didn't allow any 'rest' time in the story's forward movement. Reread your scene: were there moments of character development? Did you rush into a moment of action without properly setting it up? Did it develop fully, before it turned and reached its conclusion? You should try to be economical in writing, but you may have cut too close to the bone: each scene needs some flesh on it, too. In terms of pace, it may have rushed by a little too fast for the audience to assimilate character and story.

If your scene was much longer, did you overindulge in detail? Did you have more character development than we needed for the arc of action? Character develops across the arc of the entire play; it's not necessary to give us everything at once, or the audience will feel that your characters have become static, and lose interest. Think in terms of discovery and revelation: each new decision should reveal something extra about the character, or confirm an earlier hint. But it's also true that there are many things about a character that just aren't relevant to the particular arc of action – did you give us their life history when we didn't need that much?

Did you spend too long setting up a moment of action, stalling instead of moving on? Did you extend it unnecessarily after the action was completed? Or you may have created too much story for one scene – what you had might actually require a full play. It's a question of scale and scope.

'Arrive Late, Leave Early'

A good rule of thumb for writing the action of a scene is 'arrive late, leave early'. This means: get into the meat of the scene as swiftly as possible with the minimum necessary set-up, deliver the action and don't spin it out. Know when it's done, and move on; that way, the pace of the scene doesn't dip.

When you review your scene in light of these questions and your reader's comments, you may find that its longer or shorter length is justified; it's lean, pacy, gripping and the characters intriguing. If so, your length is correct: I gave you a target, not a prescription. If you are sure that every line of dialogue and stage direction punches its full weight, the job is well done.

5 THE THIRD PRINCIPLE: CONFLICT

In Chapters 3 and 4, movement and action emerge as two fundamental principles underpinning the structure of plays. Character status reversal, discovery and revelation, motivation and the inciting incident provide tools for you, as playwright, to set the two principles to work. But it's clear that there is very considerable similarity between the two. The distinction between them centres upon the issue of control: movement implies a series of shifts of position, but for it to function properly in drama, it has to be focused and directed. Action is the organizing process that governs movement: it supplies the necessary control.

In Chapters 5 and 6, we'll study two more principles that are also fundamental: conflict and juxtaposition, and again we'll find that they're similar but distinct. I've treated the four principles as two linked pairs for ease of discussion, but when you are writing, regard them as an interlocking quartet. It doesn't matter which of the four you decide to consider first: each one calls the other three into play as soon as you begin.

DRAWING UP THE BATTLE LINES

Hardly a day goes by without the word 'conflict' appearing in social usage. News reports update us about various 'conflicts' around the world, meaning full-scale wars, single battles or minor skirmishes. The pervasive atmosphere is one of hostility and enmity, the actions described violent and aggressive. Usually these are physical actions; but they can also be verbal combats, as in heated political exchanges. So we could add debates, quarrels, arguments, disagreements and rows to the list, shifting the emphasis from the physical level to interchanges of language.

Less heatedly, we talk about 'conflicts of interest', where it's perceived that two courses of action pull in directions that are deemed mutually detrimental. In both cases what is being described is a basic state of difference and opposition between two or more positions or conditions. But it is not a static or passive state: it is active, dynamic. Its movement creates *friction* (where the movement clashes the two together) and *rupture* (where the movement pulls the two apart.)

The state of conflict is one of relationship: the individual positions are not inherently problematic – they frequently become so only when placed in relation to each other. In another set of relationships, there might be no problem at all. So conflict is site-specific: it requires *context* and *proximity* (terms considered previously as issues of spatial organization.) Here, they help us think about the nature and degree of difference involved. If the positions are utterly unlike, they share little or no common ground or space; and thus it's harder to see where, how or why they could come into opposition with each other. So although there needs to be clear distinction between the two positions, points of similarity upon which to build some common ground – the site of dispute – are also vital. It is the active tension between similarity and difference that dynamizes the opposition. It also renders the movement pattern of conflict similarly relative in spatial terms – the opposed positions always moving towards or away from each other.

In terms of time, although we are familiar with wars lasting for long periods and family arguments perhaps spanning generations, it's worth observing that in such cases, length of time is deemed remarkable. We don't expect conflicts to continue indefinitely, and are disturbed when the end doesn't appear to be in sight. Whether or not that expectation is well-founded, we still invest emotionally, intellectually and physically in anticipating the cessation. So it appears that as well as being site-specific, conflict is also time-bound. It's conceived as a temporary rather than a permanent, open-ended state, because – largely – we regard it in negative terms, as undesirable and unsustainable. It may be, in certain circumstances, deemed to be a 'necessary evil', but our attention is nonetheless fixed upon eventual resolution and, if possible, reconciliation (the dissolution of opposites).

However, there is an exception to this question of time: the *underlying* conflict. This may be a very long-term state, even a semi-permanent one; we could point to ongoing political, military or religious disputes as examples. Within the long span of an underlying conflict will be contained many shorter and more intense localized skirmishes that build incrementally towards the slower-burning larger battle. Indeed, the sequential pattern of these recurring skirmishes, each centred around a different aspect of the underlying problem, may well be the cause

of its perpetuation. But it's still true, even of these examples, that the expectation – the hope – is that they will ultimately be time-limited by resolution and reconciliation of one kind or another (victory/defeat, compromise, settlement). So even in these cases conflict is still understood and managed as a fundamentally temporary state; renewed fighting is frequently the source of much disillusion and disappointment. The inherent finiteness of conflict gives it both a characteristic shape, and an emotional charge.

This gives us our final useful element: a goal. Conflict is motivated by the desire to achieve a particular goal or outcome; what causes conflict between the two positions is an irreconcilable mismatch between their intended goals. The mismatch often occurs because the goals are very different, but the strongest form occurs where the goals are identical but exclusive in terms of achievement. In Part B of your last exercise, that's what you were invited to find: something both women wanted but only one could have, and could only achieve at the other's expense. In other words, you brought the women into conflict, and created a winner and a loser.

Let's recap before proceeding. Conflict is a basic state of opposition between two or more positions or conditions. The state is relative, requiring the different positions to share some common – disputed – ground. It is a temporary state, that is actively moving towards goals or outcomes; sadly, those goals, which are separately held by the different positions, cannot all be accommodated. The movement involved produces friction or rupture, depending upon whether the pattern of movement brings the positions towards each other or pushes them away. Conflict can occur at the level of physical action and/ or at the level of language.

A Conflict Checklist

To help you locate and develop conflict in your play, ask:

- What are the two positions or conditions?
- What is similar about them? (the common ground)
- What is different? (the source of opposition) (It's fruitful to create more similarities than differences, but ensure that the differences are fundamental and crucial: 'deal-breakers')
- What are their goals? (Ideally, make them identical, or very similar, but mutually exclusive)
- How do they each go about pursuing their goals? What do they do? (This is where identical goals will diverge: the two sides may want the same thing, but they will each go after it in different ways)
- How much time do they have within which to achieve their goals? (Make it a tight time limit: the shorter the time period, the greater the degree of compression and intensification – time raises the stakes)
- How and why do they collide in the same space at the same time? (How are you going to bring the collision onstage?)

THE FOUR PRINCIPLES: TEAMWORK

It's clear that conflict is valuable as a dramatic principle that interacts with both movement and action. Character status reversal, that orchestrates movement and provides a unit of action, is inherently conflict-based. The process of action throws high and low status together, creating friction; this reaches crisis point and detonates, driving them forcibly apart (rupture) into new, reversed, positions. Discovery and revelation can also serve as tools for creating conflict, since there is an inherent opposition between ignorance and knowledge, lack and gain. (We noted, too, the value of opposites in construction: secrets, concealment, failure to recognize and refusal to acknowledge working in conflict with discovery, revelation, recognition and acknowledgement.)

The patterns of conflict outlined above are patterns that motivate the arc of dramatic action. Many script analysts insist that they are essential to render a play properly dramatic. 'Where is the action? There's no conflict.' is a common criticism. And lastly, the inciting incident, the disruption that tips the opening balance into movement, starts the process of bringing the two opposed positions into collision. It therefore sets up the first flashpoint of conflict.

It should be apparent, too, that conflict is also inseparable from juxtaposition (which literally means placing two things side by side.) Until the two positions are placed side by side (within the space of common ground), there is no possibility of friction, because there is no relationship. It is the process of juxtaposition itself which therefore activates the conflict. Just as action is a process of organising movement, so juxtaposition is a process of organizing conflict: the two pairs at work with each other.

But if we work across the pairs, we can see that the two processes are linked: action, as a causal *sequence*, works by dint of juxtaposition, one element after another; and conversely, the process of bringing elements into a juxtaposed relationship is itself an arc of action. Conflict is, by definition, constantly in motion; movement from and towards fixed points is often both the cause of conflict and also its effect (friction and rupture). When conflict stops moving, it ceases to be conflict: it becomes merely the potential for conflict, or its aftermath.

In terms of the six basic questions, conflict naturally responds to what? (what happens?) But because of its site-specific and time-bound nature, it also responds to where? and when? – it requires you to think about the space of common ground and temporary duration.

Conflict is goal-orientated by nature. The goal itself may be ill-defined, or possibly not yet defined at the outset: for example, does a small child, instructed not to touch a hot object, actually understand his goal in stretching out his hand to disobey? Nonetheless, there still is a goal: satisfaction of curiosity, acquisition of knowledge, assertion of his will over his parent's, perhaps. In some circumstances – often, in underlying conflicts of long duration – the original goal can appear to have become subsumed, by habit, into resistance for resistance's sake. In these instances, the conflict has become its own objective, and continuing to fight brings its own satisfaction. Thus, the goal-orientation of conflict responds to the question why?

Pause here, and look back: in the discussion so far, what – or rather who – has not yet been mentioned?

CONFLICT AND CHARACTER

Character (that responds to who?) has not yet been mentioned. I've taken care so far to describe conflict as a state of difference between two or more 'positions' or 'conditions', rather than as an opposition between characters.

A dramatic character is more than just an individual; it is the physical embodiment of the play's themes, the primary vessel that carries your play's intended communication with your audience. (Depending upon the kind of play you want to write, your characters may or may not be human beings.) Conflict occurs above and beyond the level of individual character: it occurs across the human spectrum, at the level of race, gender, belief, value systems, for example; and also between, and within, the human, natural and supernatural worlds.

But we know that the strongest form of dramatic action is rooted in characters who are recognizably motivated by powerful human drives; so too, the strongest form of conflict occurs between characters. Within the boundaries of individual characters, we can compress the scope of broader conflicts, and through compression, create intensification. Characters have to embody and transmit the essence of the broader conflict, to conceive and act out the pursuit of goals, experience the collisions, friction and rupture that may actually be occurring in a much wider spectrum. And in doing so, they once again function as metaphors: carriers of multilayered meaning. That is, they not only fight their own personal battles, they wrestle with *all* of the battles, as two champions might take on single combat to end a larger dispute.

To explore character as metaphoric 'combatant', let's look at four major adversarial *character functions*: four particular sets of tasks assigned within the process of dramatic storytelling:

- protagonist
- antagonist
- ally
- opponent

Protagonist is another term derived from Greek drama. It refers to the central character, whom we often call the 'hero' (used here to mean a male or female character). *Antagonist* derives from the same source. In everyday language, when we're talking about heroes, we usually also talk about villains: 'the hero of the hour', 'the villain of the piece'. But there's a slippage of vocabulary here: whilst a villain in a play will usually fulfil the function of the antagonist, it's not necessarily true that every antagonist is a villain. (That is, not all antagonists are bad; and likewise, not all protagonists are good, so they aren't all heroes in the noble sense.)

If we set the two terms alongside each other (prot/agon/ist, ant/agon/ist) – it's obvious that they share a common core, the Greek *agon*, which means contest or argument. So at the

---

Dramatic Function v. Moral Nature

There are moralistic overtones to 'hero' and 'villain' that can limit your thinking about characters. It's better to separate the character's moral nature (hero/ villain) from its dramatic function (protagonist/ antagonist), so that you will have a wider variety of combinations at your fingertips. You could have:

- a protagonist who is heroic
- a protagonist who is villainous
- a morally upstanding antagonist
- an antagonist who is completely reprehensible.

Shuffle these variations and you can have the following possibilities to play with:

- 'good' protagonist v. 'bad' antagonist
- 'good' protagonist v. 'good' antagonist
- 'bad' protagonist v. 'bad' antagonist
- 'bad' protagonist v. 'good' antagonist

---

very heart of both character functions is the notion of conflict: their joint role is to pursue the contest. To the protagonist falls the task of carrying forward the argument, to the antagonist, the task of blocking or opposing it. But until each one carries out his function, there is no true agon – no contest. They have to be brought together, and thus although the protagonist is the central character, the antagonist is a component of equal importance.

Identifying the Protagonist

When I've spoken about 'your story', it's been in reference to the entire arc of your play. But each character within the play should have her own unique story, that gives her an arc of movement throughout. This is important because audiences develop their understanding of characters by comparing and contrasting them with one another, and so you need to have a number of available aspects for them to use. Developing a detailed individual story for each character provides you with the source material for comparison and contrast.

There will, however, be one character's story that dominates the others, and it is the telling of this story that shapes the arc of the play overall. This is the story that carries most of the weight of the play's argument; this is the character we follow most closely, to whom our sympathies are drawn (possibly willingly, possibly reluctantly.) It is the protagonist's story, and it should be the strongest one of all. When you are developing your characters, find the one with the strongest, most active story: that character should be your protagonist. If you find that your intended protagonist doesn't have the strongest story, you should realign the play to follow the character who does. Sometimes, that shift of focus can be the making of a play that is stumbling and stalling.

The 'Doubled' or Group Protagonist

Can there be more than one protagonist? Perhaps you want to write a 'will they/ won't they?' romantic comedy about a couple (a 'doubled' protagonist), or you want to write about a group of people. 'Protagonist' is the term for a dramatic function, rather than a specific character; it's at its clearest when the function is enacted by a single character, but it can also be shared.

Think of the couple or the group as a *single unit*, collectively carrying out the function of protagonist. Each character within the unit will have his own story; the strongest story, however, belongs to the unit itself. It's the story of the group or couple, about what they share.

Building the Antagonist

The second strongest story is the antagonist's. Her task is to block or oppose the protagonist's forward progress; she creates obstacles that complicate the action, leading to the crisis and climax. The antagonist is vital: until she appears and embarks upon her task, there is no conflict. She is its catalyst. In terms of movement, status reversal emerges as a key feature. From the first block thrown up by the antagonist, the protagonist advances in a series of falls and rises; for him, each successful block is a fall, while each block overcome is a rise, until the crisis – his lowest moment. Then, in the climax, he reverses the lowest fall, and rises to the resolution. But from the antagonist's point of view, the inverse is true: each successful block is, for her, a rise, whilst every block overcome by the protagonist is a fall. The crisis is, for her, the pinnacle – and then the status is reversed, and the resolution

reached. Antagonists, therefore, usually end on a descending note.

Building a good antagonist is in many ways more complex than creating a protagonist. Through comparison and contrast, the specific nature of the antagonist serves to develop the audience's deeper understanding of the protagonist. So what you are actually doing, when you work on your antagonist, is increasing the complexity of your central character, too.

The antagonist's dramatic task is to block the protagonist's progress, but if that is all she does, the arc of action falls into a very repetitive stop-start pattern, with a jerky rhythm and little or no suspense. There is no real sense that the antagonist is a genuine match for the protagonist, and we don't see a real contest between them. The antagonist must create suspense by convincing us that she is capable of defeating the protagonist; not only blocking his progress, but destroying it altogether. In the arc of dramatic action, she should very nearly achieve this destruction. Then we have a real battle on our hands, building along a rising arc.

In Chapter 4, the image/ shadow method helped develop the opening and final balances of the story, and locate the inciting incident. And in working out how to motivate the play's action, we calibrated the character drives of desire, fear and need. These two methods can help you again here; since the two characters mutually inform one another, they should be developed in tandem. Develop your profiles of the protagonist and antagonist on facing pages of your notebook. Begin by giving to the antagonist the shadow version of every image detail you give to the protagonist. Similarly, with the drives of desire, fear and need, make the protagonist's desires what the antagonist fears, and vice versa. This is the most basic level of construction: they are the absolute antithesis of each other.

For the purposes of conflict, though, some common ground is essential, and at the moment there doesn't appear to be any. There are no points of comparison, only contrasts. But because one is the complete inverse of the other, they do have a relationship: as opposites, they have the potential for conflict within them. Re-examine each detail in its image and shadow form: is there any common ground between the two versions? For example, if the protagonist is a woman who believes that all human life is sacred, the antagonist, in the shadow form, would be a man who thinks that all human life is expendable. The common ground here is that they both have an active attitude towards human life: an attitude they would be prepared to act upon. Immediately, in terms of action, that provides a means of bringing them into collision: place a human life in jeopardy and confront both the protagonist and antagonist with a need to respond. If it is a human life that has significance to both parties, the stakes are raised even higher (it may have quite a different significance for each, though). A still greater challenge to both characters might be to make the life at risk either the protagonist's or the antagonist's.

BALANCING SIMILARITY AND DIFFERENCE

You can develop a more rounded and absorbing protagonist/antagonist pair by complicating the balance of similarity/difference. Look at your two lists of details again. What might be the implications of switching a few pairs of details around, so that the protagonist and antagonist both have some image and some shadow detail? You will find you're developing both strengths and weaknesses in the two character functions; but because they are always developed in pairs, the area of strength in one will always find the matching area of vulnerability in the other.

'Common Ground' and the Emotional Arc

It's likely that, in teasing out the underlying common ground (the similarities beneath the apparent discrepancies), you will find that the shared element often addresses issues of considerable substance. These derive from the themes of your play that express what your story is really about. In building your protagonist and antagonist, identifying what they both share will contribute substantially to the emotional arc of your story. Identifying what is unique to each (what they don't share) will help you begin to work through the physical arc of the story: a series of opportunities for clashes over what is shared.

This is an excellent means of avoiding the jerky stop–start pattern of progress and block: now you can make the antagonist equally active. Both protagonist and antagonist will naturally always try to play to their own strengths; since one's strength is the other's weakness, whoever gains the upper hand forces the other to retreat. But if the reactive partner resists and pushes back, the action is poised: will it continue again in the same direction or will it pivot, turning former strength into new weakness, throwing progress into retreat?

There is another benefit to be derived from redistributing image and shadow details across the pair. Each character will acquire a combination of positive and negative elements. As well as positive and negative coming into conflict across the pair, the two sets of elements can also come into conflict within the individual characters. This can really help to deepen the two characters; they are not just fighting each other – at critical moments, they will also probably be fighting themselves. So the conflict pattern of collision, friction and rupture will be occuring within, as well as between, the two characters. In this way, exploring the dramatic *function* also provides you with a means of developing unique individual characters to carry them out.

This is the best way to build an antagonist: build her in as much detail, make her as powerful and complex, as the protagonist. Send her out to pursue her own set of goals equally actively, but make the goals of each party incompatible. Instead of complete antithesis, we now have a much subtler version: they are a match, a reciprocating mirror. One has what the other lacks, one knows what the other doesn't, one can do what the other can't. The audience thus has a very rich mix of aspects for comparison and contrast.

ADDING TO THE CHARACTER MIX

Protagonist and antagonist square up to each other in various forms and degrees of combat throughout the play. But essentially, it's another repeated pattern – one-to-one encounters – and the variations are not endless. To expand the possible range of conflict patterns, add a second, subsidiary, pair of character functions: 'ally' and 'opponent'.

EXERCISE
What do you notice about these two terms? What possible combinations or variations can you see?

COMMENTS
They contain implied opposites: the ally of one party becomes the opponent of the other party. This can be a means of multiplying characters: both protagonist and antagonist could each have a 'sidekick'. To minimize confusion, call the protagonist's sidekick the 'ally', and the antagonist's sidekick the 'opponent'. But note that the two sidekicks do, in fact, fulfil both functions simultaneously: the protagonist's ally is also the antagonist's opponent; the protagonist's opponent is, at the same time, the antagonist's ally. Two more characters, but they widen the range of possible situation combinations:

- Protagonist v. antagonist (1 v. 1)
- Ally v. opponent (1 v. 1)
- Protagonist v. opponent (1 v. 1)
- Ally v. antagonist (1 v. 1)
- Protagonist + ally v. antagonist (2 v. 1)
- Protagonist + ally v. opponent (2 v. 1)
- Protagonist v. antagonist + opponent (1 v. 2)
- Ally v. antagonist + opponent (1 v. 2)
- Protagonist + ally v. antagonist + opponent (2 v. 2)

There are hybrid variations, too:

Ally-opponent
This might be someone who begins as the protagonist's ally, turns into his opponent temporarily, then reverts to being an ally again. The temporary opposition will probably be reluctant, but could be willing. Or she begins as an ally then turns into a permanent opponent, perhaps in protest, perhaps because she has been corrupted.

Opponent-ally
This is the reverse: someone who begins as the protagonist's opponent (reluctantly or willingly) turns into a temporary ally, then reverts back. Or he may permanently convert into an ally.

False ally (underlying opponent)

This would be someone who appears to be the protagonist's ally, but is really covertly an opponent. His true function will ultimately be revealed by the play's action.

False opponent (underlying ally)

This is someone who appears to be the protagonist's opponent but is really covertly an ally. Her true function will ultimately be revealed by the play's action.

Notice that ally-opponent/false ally and opponent-ally/false opponent are not necessarily the same thing. An ally-opponent is genuinely an ally who then becomes a genuine opponent. A false ally is a deceiver, faking it until exposed.

Notice, too, that the terms are 'ally' and 'opponent', not 'friend' and 'enemy'. As with hero and villain, friend and enemy have emotional and perhaps moral overtones, so they can be manipulated to offer additional variations:

- an ally who is also a friend (this intensifies the alliance)
- an opponent who is also an enemy (this intensifies the opposition)
- an ally who is also an enemy (perhaps a reluctant ally, such as a hostile witness in a court case; or a reluctant enemy: a divorcing couple fighting a custody battle, perhaps?)
- an opponent who is also a friend (a reluctant opponent, such as the best friend who tells the protagonist her dress makes her look awful, or a reluctant friend: this could be the best friend who falls in love with the protagonist's partner)

These four character functions help you initiate and develop conflict. The subsidiary pair are valuable because unlike the protagonist and antagonist, they can change

sides and unbalance any given situation. But their primary function is to help deepen the audience's understanding of the protagonist and antagonist: use the image/shadow and desire/ fear/ need detail lists to help develop these relationships. This becomes interesting in that the patterns of similarity and difference are now distributed four ways instead of just two: you should therefore find yourself dealing in rather subtler degrees of distinction.

Remember that all the functions can be performed by single characters, or by several characters collectively. If a function is performed by more than one character, keep your eye on the function itself, and think of the multiple characters in terms of a unit. Be careful not to create too many characters, though: you could risk losing control of the arc of the central conflict.

TWO IN ONE

There is one set of variations to the protagonist/antagonist, ally/opponent pairings not yet considered, that builds upon the potential for creating conflict within the individual character himself. They occur when a character combines two functions.

In *The Beauty Queen of Leenane*, it is Maureen's story we follow (she is, as the dialogue signals, the 'beauty queen'). She is the protagonist, which makes Mag the antagonist. But the strength and ambiguity of the relationship McDonagh creates between the two women and, in particular, the twist that reveals Maureen's history of violence towards Mag, complicates the attribution of function. Maureen is as much Mag's antagonist as Mag is hers. It is really the *pair* which is the true protagonist, and thus also the *pair* which is the true antagonist. In the final sequence, when Maureen's violence towards Mag is unleashed, Mag is destroyed. Maureen is faced with living out the shadow form of the opening balance detail: 'Maureen lives alone'. But she cannot. Her habitual war with Mag – an underlying conflict – is so ingrained that she ends the play sitting in Mag's rocking chair, listening to the radio, just as Mag did in the opening image of the play. Maureen had a previous history of mental illness, and perhaps her mind has now given way. She has fully 'internalized' her antagonist at this point.

When this occurs – the combination of protagonist and antagonist within the same 'body' – it's very absorbing and unsettling. In such cases, the protagonist is her own nemesis (the source of her own destruction), and the resolution leaves her literally or figuratively ripped apart.

The protagonist can also be his own constant opponent, without being his own ultimate antagonist. In *Hamlet*, for example, Hamlet's antagonist is Claudius, his uncle and the murderer of Hamlet's father. The course of the play's action steadily brings them into collision, until the final battle between them. But until the last scene, Hamlet's own intellect and moral conscience repeatedly oppose his emotional drive to take immediate revenge on Claudius, creating a series of delays and complications. It is often this protagonist/ opponent combination that allows you to exploit the internal divisions within the character created by the mixture of image and shadow detail.

We can examine the possibilities of the protagonist, antagonist, ally and opponent character functions in a sample play.

BLUE/ORANGE (2000)

In Joe Penhall's *Blue/Orange*, Christopher is a young black man who has been arrested and placed in a state-run psychiatric hospital for evaluation and treatment under a compulsory 28-day detention order. As the play begins, Christopher is reaching the end of the period and eagerly expecting his release. He has been under the care of Dr Bruce Flaherty, a young doctor in training with ambitions to become a psychiatric registrar. Bruce has grave reservations about Christopher's suitability for release; he believes him to be a paranoid schizophrenic and wants to retain him in hospital for his own safety and further treatment. But in order to do so, Bruce requires his diagnosis to be confirmed by his medical supervisor, Dr Robert Smith, who is senior consultant and the department's head. The play consists of just these three characters, and takes place over the course of one day, in a hospital consulting room.

Christopher is the site of conflict: the two doctors disagree totally about his condition and the best course of action. Bruce wants to retain him, Robert, to release him. Bruce believes that Christopher is seriously mentally ill; Robert believes his condition to be 'within normal boundaries' given his race and the particular social circumstances that young black British men face. But very quickly, the battle shifts gear and becomes a fight for personal supremacy between Bruce and Robert, and Christopher is drawn into taking sides.

The conflict pattern is clearly set up: the two positions are quite distinct, and it's obvious where the differences lie. The common ground is an agreement that Christopher has a mental condition that deviates from the accepted norm; although Robert believes it to be the product of social circumstances, he definitely envisages that Christopher will need continuing treatment. Unlike Bruce, however, he believes this can be handled on an out-patient basis. And of course there are other similarities: both are psychiatrists, both know the 'rules of evidence' in determining mental illness or health. Both have aspirations to advance their careers – Bruce to become a specialist registrar, Robert to become a

Professor – and both see Christopher's diagnosis and treatment as a means of furthering their ambitions.

The time clock is running from the outset: the compulsory 28-day detention order under which Christopher was committed to the hospital has twenty-four hours left to run, and then Christopher must either be released or be subject to a new order. This is why Bruce and Robert collide: Bruce needs Robert to agree to the new order. It also determines the place in which the collision occurs – the consulting room – and the initial territory of conflict: it's a professional disagreement.

Looking at the distribution of functions amongst the three characters, it's clear immediately that the ally and opponent functions would have to be performed by one character, since the play is a three-hander. We meet Christopher and Bruce first; Robert arrives later. Though it's not unheard-of for the protagonist to be introduced after the antagonist, it's more rare: so it's not likely that Penhall intends Robert to be the protagonist. He could therefore either be the antagonist or could combine the ally and opponent functions.

EXERCISE
• If Robert is the antagonist, who is the protagonist? Whose progress does Robert actively oppose?
• Who therefore functions as both ally and opponent to the protagonist?

COMMENTS
• Robert actively blocks Bruce's goal of retaining Christopher in hospital; this places Bruce in the role of protagonist. That would make Bruce's the dominant story, and Bruce the character to whom our sympathies should therefore be drawn.
• Christopher would thus be the character who combines the two functions of ally and opponent.

This works well: it means Christopher can switch sides, and when he does so, he creates a 2 v. 1 imbalance. He can switch function more than once, and thus can bring about status reversals between Bruce and Robert.

Penhall achieves the switches very well, using two objects as the pivot points. The first is an orange that, in Act One, Christopher insists is blue, both inside and outside. This would seem to support Bruce's doubts, since we can see for ourselves that the orange isn't blue. Robert, however, suggests that Christopher might simply be using the term as a simile, and cites a poem and a comic book that both employ the term. He proposes that Christopher, who claims to be the son of the former Ugandan President Idi Amin, may even have encountered these writings. Bruce rejects this idea, pointing to both of Christopher's claims as clear proof of his delusional condition.

The second object is a newspaper cutting about Idi Amin, that Christopher keeps as a talisman. He shows it to Robert in Act Two. Intriguingly, the article contains references to East African oranges, and Amin's eighteen children by five different women – one of whom, the article claims, is now living in London. This throws a different light on Christopher's claims. And it emerges, in conversation with Robert, that Christopher's job is selling fruit on a market stall – he *sells* oranges, which, of course, turn a nasty shade of blue as they rot. (Christopher claimed, in Act One, that the 'blue' orange was 'a bad orange. Don't eat it.') So there's now a distinct possibility that Christopher may have a rational basis for both his claims.

These two objects – the orange and the newspaper cutting – that can be read in opposing ways, switch Christopher between functions. In Act One, they seem to support Bruce's contention that the young man is delusional: Christopher's statements make

91

him Bruce's ally. But in Act Two, where Christopher gives Robert (Bruce's antagonist) a possible rational explanation for his claims, he is equipping Robert to block Bruce's progress: he has switched functions, becoming Robert's ally and Bruce's opponent.

Penhall uses this 'switching capacity' of Christopher's, pivoting around the two objects, to raise the pitch of the battle between Bruce and Robert. As psychiatrists, both men interpret the language and behaviour of their patients; if they interpret them identically, they will agree on a diagnosis and a treatment strategy. But if they don't agree, then the spotlight falls more acutely on the ways in which they have arrived at their different interpretations. This places Bruce and Robert under the microscope instead of Christopher: they are no longer clinically detached but personally involved, because their interpretations will reveal their own underlying attitudes and prejudices. So it's no longer simply a professional battle, it's also personal, tapping into each man's desires, fears and needs. And as Robert is of higher status than Bruce in terms of rank, it's a power battle.

In this reading, Christopher is not deliberately a false ally, or false opponent. He is not pretending. But he is, both doctors agree, suffering a degree of mental illness, which complicates the audience's (as well as Bruce's and Robert's) ability to evaluate the truth of his claims. Penhall also beautifully invokes the friend/enemy possibility, too: Robert, for example, tells Christopher that Bruce has planted ideas in his mind by leading him too strongly to claim that the orange was blue, which indeed we heard him do ('Yes but they're not *orange* oranges, are they?') This creates a suspicion in Christopher that Bruce is actually his enemy rather than his friend. And since the core of the argument between Bruce and Robert is a diagnosis of *paranoid* schizophrenia, the concepts of friend and enemy are in play throughout.

However, this attribution of functions (Bruce: protagonist, Robert: antagonist, Christopher: ally/opponent), is not the only way of reading *Blue/Orange*; they can be attributed differently, and it is this possibility that Penhall harnesses to deepen the complexity of the play's overall argument.

BLACK AND WHITE

EXERCISE
In the alternative attribution of functions:

- If Christopher becomes the protagonist, who becomes the antagonist? (Think about Christopher's goal. Who is blocking his progress towards achieving it?)
- What function does the third character perform in relation to the protagonist Christopher? Ally or opponent?
- What might be some of the implications for our understanding of the overall story created by this new attribution of functions?

COMMENTS
- When the remaining twenty-four hours of his detention order expire, Christopher wants to get out of the hospital. Bruce is trying to prevent him from leaving (because he believes he is seriously ill and a danger to himself.) Christopher can't leave without Bruce's consent, and so Bruce is absolutely blocking any progress towards Christopher's goal. He is functioning as Christopher's antagonist. In terms of the way Penhall first introduces the three characters, Christopher and Bruce 'stand facing each other'. We could see this as, literally, a confrontational 'face-off' from the word go. The first line is spoken by Christopher, so it is Christopher, not Bruce, to whom we turn first.

- Robert is the third character. Since his goal throughout is to release the patient, he clearly functions as Christopher's ally (and is therefore Bruce's opponent.) Though he sometimes wavers slightly in his diagnosis, he becomes personally invested in the young man's release; so it's harder to see him as Christopher's opponent. However, Christopher does keep saying and doing things that undermine Robert's confidence in his sanity (making it harder for Robert to overrule Bruce and order his release.) So we could attribute the opponent function to Christopher: like Hamlet, the protagonist's mental state creates his own set of obstacles towards achieving his desired goal.

- If Christopher is the protagonist, then he is intended to attract the audience's sympathies. His is the dominant story, the story of a young black British man who has been arrested for disruptive public behaviour and committed to a psychiatric hospital. He is compelled to prove his sanity in order to win his release; if he fails to do so, he will be adjudged to be mentally ill, and could be subject to a much longer period of compulsory detention. His freedom is therefore at stake.

Christopher is black British: Bruce and Robert are white British. It is this distinction that unsettles the play. Both Bruce and Robert, in their professional disagreement, appeal to what I referred to above as an 'accepted norm' of sanity: that is, they agree upon a set of criteria by which a person's behaviour might be judged rational or irrational. And they both agree that by these criteria, Christopher's behaviour is irrational. What they disagree about is the root cause. Bruce believes it to be illness. Robert attributes its eccentricities to Christopher's social experience of endemic racism ('Women on escalators holding their handbags that little bit tighter as you pass.

People looking straight through you as if you're not even there. Football hooligans. Skinheads. Throwing bananas.') Bruce and Robert are apparently reading Christopher's behaviour within different, but adjacent, contexts.

But if Christopher is the protagonist, for him the primary site of conflict is not really the interpretations of his behaviour adduced by the two doctors. His primary conflict is with the definition of the 'accepted norm' of sanity – of which both doctors agree he falls foul. But who selects the defining criteria? Who validates the definition, and upon what basis? In this play, it is Bruce and Robert (as representatives of the medical establishment) – but both men have a personal investment in the outcome, so it might be argued that their objectivity is compromised. Does Christopher's race have relevance? Bruce does not, initially, signal that it is a factor in his response. Robert does. In fact, Christopher's case offers him, he believes, a golden opportunity to build upon his research publication (on the roots of delusion in specific cultural backgrounds) and to secure his Professorship on the back of discovering, as he phrases it, 'A "cure" for "black psychosis"'.

Robert is 'seeing' Christopher, first and foremost, as black: he believes that this is the source of Christopher's problem. Bruce 'sees' Christopher, first and foremost, as sick: he believes that this is the source of the problem. But as the play progresses, if we follow Christopher in the function of protagonist, it becomes disturbingly apparent that perhaps neither man is genuinely seeing Christopher at all. They are both too strongly invested in attaching labels and categories to him *as an object* – just as the orange and the newspaper clipping are capable of being appropriated to either side of the argument, so Christopher is constantly under appropriation.

At this level of meaning, Robert, as well as

Bruce, is really functioning as Christopher's antagonist. Robert certainly does fulfil the ally function of helping Christopher achieve his goal – he is released by the end of the play. But if we have listened carefully throughout to the bandying of terms and definitions, and picked up the verbal slippages that occur (such as the twisting and turning of loaded terms such as 'uppity nigga' and 'voodoo'), we are no longer fully able to determine whether or not this is a good thing. We can't feel comfortable either with the interpretation of 'accepted norm' criteria made by Bruce and Robert, or with the criteria themselves. All seems compromised, and we are left with a sense that Christopher has been badly served.

By allowing us the possibility of reading Christopher rather than Bruce as the protagonist, Penhall is able to activate all the fault lines and disturbances in contemporary society about the issue of race. In doing so, he dramatizes an underlying societal conflict by means of a series of shorter, more intense localized skirmishes.

Penhall's use of the play's structure itself as a substantial carrier of the overall argument is what makes *Blue/Orange* excellent writing. When I first saw the play, I assumed that Bruce was the protagonist (the first distribution of functions); I found myself influenced by the basic situation into responding to Christopher as an object of investigation. But on teasing out the alternative distribution of functions and the meanings it makes available, it became clear that my assumption was, in a profound way, what the play was about. This is a splendid example of a play having the capacity to continue 'cooking' after the performance ends.

SCRIPT EXERCISE

Each situation in the following list has the potential for conflict. Choose one.

Situations:

- A few people are in an elevator. It suddenly stops between floors.
- A young bride and her husband arrive home from their honeymoon. His mother meets them at the door of their brand new home.
- In the depths of a snow blizzard, a young man's journey home is suddenly halted. It is after midnight, and the temperature is well below freezing.

If none of these situations appeals, you could look through a newspaper for some suggestions. Brief page-filler items, about three or four lines long, could be a good source: the brevity of the item usually means that the sub-editor will have summarized the situation and identified one or two key details, but that's all you will have to go on. You can be free to invent the scope of the conflict yourself. Make sure you choose an item that suggests the potential for conflict.

To allow room for characters and conflict to develop, aim for six to eight pages of script.

Try not to rush into writing the scene until you have structured it properly. Although this is an exercise to help you explore technique, think about what you would really like to discuss with your audience through this scene. Allow it to carry something personal, and distinctive of you.

Keep your first draft of the scene simple and direct; concentrate on the quality of the characters, and the clarity of the story arc. Further, perhaps longer, versions of the scene can be used to complicate the action, introduce more characters, split or combine functions.

Give the scene to your reader for feedback. You want to know what they think is happening; whether or not it's believable; where it becomes confused. Ask them which

Exercise checklist

- Use *A conflict checklist* to help you develop the conflict. Consider whether the conflict is between characters, between character and situation, or between human character and non-human environment.
- Use the functions of protagonist, antagonist, ally and opponent to plot the arc of your characters through the conflict.
- Take plenty of time to develop the characters by means of the image/ shadow method, and identify the drives of desire, need and fear. Make the characters as rich and rounded as you can.
- Use status reversal, discovery and revelation as tools to help you create movement.
- Plan the complete arc of action: establish the opening balance; find the inciting incident and the character decision it precipitates.
- Give your characters strong, active but contradictory goals.
- Outline the series of rises and falls, progress and blocks that take the scene through to its crisis, climax, resolution and closing balance.

structure. Try to draw from the points questions that you can ask about the scene. It's hard, at first, to be sufficiently detached from the script draft to be able to see where it works and where it doesn't, but this critical skill is one you need to cultivate. It's as much a part of the process of becoming a good playwright as is the writing of dialogue and stage directions.

Be honest: find where you might have cut corners in the planning stages, or where you fell into clichés of character and situation. But also look for places where you might have overindulged yourself, been too elaborate or complicated in your plotting, or included superfluous elements of character detail. In particular, be quite ruthless with the dialogue and the stage directions: was there more of each than was really needed? Is the dialogue, especially, a bit florid and 'purple'? Does it get in the way of the scene's ability to communicate with the audience, rather than promoting it?

Aim for:

- Simplicity
- Economy
- Clarity
- Meaning
- Feeling

character(s) they found interesting, and why. Who did they think was the main character? Check the pacing and rhythm of the scene: did they find it rushed, or too slow? Could they guess how it was going to turn out? Did they feel it turned out the 'right' way? Why? (Or why not?)

COMMENTS

On the basis of your reader's comments, review the scene yourself. Use the worklist of planning and development points above as the basis for testing the strength of the scene

When you've completed your review and wielded the editing pencil, ask yourself, before tackling the rewrite: what is there of me in this scene? Remember that audiences are always listening to pick up the distinctive notes of the playwright's own unique voice. Make sure they're there, in your scene.

Now, armed with your reader's comments and your own critical notes, rewrite the draft and improve it. Address *only* the aspects that didn't work as well as they should have. Leave the successful aspects alone: you could spoil a good thing. As the saying goes, 'if it ain't broke, don't fix it.'

95

6 THE FOURTH PRINCIPLE: JUXTAPOSITION

SUBVERTING EXPECTATIONS

Restaurant. Table set for dinner with white tablecloth. Six places. MARLENE *and* WAITRESS.

EXERCISE
This is the opening stage direction of *Top Girls*, by Caryl Churchill.

*   What information does it suggest about the scene which will follow?
*   Use the six questions: where? when? who? what? why? how? to help you work out what is being set in motion.
*   If you already know the play, try not to cheat! Work with this information only: this is the visual image that the audience receives, in performance.

COMMENTS
From the moment the stage lights rise on this opening image, the audience starts to sift the evidence, predicting answers to at least some of the six basic questions.

*   *Where?* isn't a problem, though the restaurant's location isn't yet known. But it's an interior scene, taking place in a public setting.
*   There's no indication of a period setting, so it's likely that *when?* is the present day. It's evening (table set for dinner) but of which day, or whether that's going to be important to the story, are yet to emerge.

*   *Who* is Marlene? It appears that she's in charge of what's happening, which seems to be a private dinner for six people. So she's the host, and her five guests are due to arrive.
*   The exact nature of the event (*what?*) isn't certain: private dinners could be formal or informal, between friends, relatives or business associates. It could be a birthday party, or some other kind of celebration. There aren't any downbeat signs – nothing draped in black crêpe to suggest a funeral wake, for example – so it seems to be an upbeat occasion.
*   *Why?* We don't yet know why Marlene is hosting a dinner.
*   *How?* addresses the storytelling method. Everything appears very realistic, so it's probably going to unfold according to the kinds of causally structured patterns explored thus far. That seems to be confirmed by the style of the dialogue and action that follows:

MARLENE. Excellent, yes, table for six. One of them's going to be late but we won't wait. I'd like a bottle of Frascati straight away if you've got one really cold.
The WAITRESS *goes.*
ISABELLA BIRD *arrives.*
Here we are. Isabella.
ISABELLA. Congratulations, my dear.
MARLENE. Well, it's a step. It makes for a party.

It's at this point that Churchill begins to subvert expectations, for Isabella Bird is in Victorian costume. She could be in fancy dress, but if it's that kind of party, why isn't Marlene in costume, too? Hard on Isabella's heels, three more characters arrive: Nijo, in full Japanese kimono, Gret, in armour, and Joan in ecclesiastical robes. The five women sit down, drink, chat, order dinner just as predicted, but there isn't any reference to their striking appearance, which seems rather odd. Also odd is the content and particular idiom of each guest's conversation. Isabella and Nijo both talk about travel: Isabella's voyages are catalogues of great physical hardship and Christian suffering. There is a pervading sense of 'mission' about them. They don't chime with our sense that this is a contemporary setting, appearing instead to refer to an earlier historical time. Nijo's stories are startling: she describes becoming the Emperor's lover at the age of fourteen, her fall from favour and subsequent pilgrimage, on foot, throughout Japan. She talks with precise formality about multilayered silk gowns, the protocols of sake-drinking, and rigid sexual etiquette.

Joan chips in with an account of living disguised as a man, in order to achieve an education in Athens and a glorious career as a theological scholar in Rome, followed by her eventual election as Pope. She recounts – in graphic detail that is at first hilarious – the public scandal of her pregnancy, giving birth in the street during a Papal procession, and her subsequent stoning to death by a mob outside the city walls. In the ensuing silence that returns to raucous laughter as she tells of the cardinals' outraged attempts to ensure such a blasphemy could never again occur, Griselda, the sixth (late) dinner guest arrives. In full medieval costume.

Marlene introduces everyone, and the remarkable nature of what is happening is spelt out:

MARLENE. Now who do you know? This is Joan who was Pope in the ninth century, and Isabella Bird, the Victorian traveller, and Lady Nijo from Japan, Emperor's concubine and Buddhist nun, thirteenth century, nearer your own time, and Gret who was painted by Brueghel. Griselda's in Boccaccio and Petrarch and Chaucer because of her extraordinary marriage.

Though we're looking at what appears to be a realistic contemporary scene of six women enjoying a communal celebration dinner, five of the women derive from different historical time periods, art and medieval literature. They are, in the realistic sense, impossible. Yet here they are.

When *Top Girls* received its premiere in 1982 at the Royal Court Theatre in London, reviewers were not immediately sure how to respond. Caryl Churchill was criticized in some reviews for the structure of the play; it was suggested in one or two that *Top Girls* wasn't actually a 'proper' play at all, because it didn't follow the arc of causal development that is still very much the dominant form. The progression of scenes, the organization of time and space, and the approach to character all seemed not to follow any of the traditional patterns. Dialogue, instead of being spoken in alternate sequence (we are accustomed to hearing theatrical characters speak in turn), overlapped and interrupted itself. At times, several of the women were speaking at once, which meant that not every word spoken was distinguishable. But since 1982, the play has justifiably come to be regarded as a landmark piece of innovative and truly theatrical writing. Its influence can be traced in the work of many of the most exciting British playwrights of the last decade, such as Mark Ravenhill, Sarah Kane, Martin Crimp, and Abi Morgan. The techniques it employs also underpin internationally renowned theatre works such as Tony Kushner's *Angels in America* plays (*Millennium Approaches* and *Perestroika*), and productions by the French-Canadian writer/director/actor Robert Lepage.

Top Girls provides a model for exploration of the fourth fundamental principle: juxtaposition. Its bold employment of this principle opens up alternative strategies for play structure to the causal patterns studied earlier. This doesn't mean, however, that Churchill does not employ the principles of movement, action and conflict. She does, but at every turn, her use challenges our habitual expectations about them. Nor does it mean that juxtaposition cannot be harnessed to deliver familiar causal patterns. It not only can, it must be: without it, there cannot be any conflict, for example. But in this chapter, juxtaposition shows how plays can be thrillingly written from a completely fresh starting point.

BANKING ENERGY

Juxtaposition is the process of constructing relationships between dramatic components. It creates a framework of coherence around them. Within this context, the audience is invited to contemplate the components from a point of view that could be familiar or unconventional, or perhaps from a series of shifting points of view. By the simple act of placing two elements next to one another on stage, attention is focused upon them, as if in a form of cinematic 'close-up'. We are provoked into attributing meaning not only to the separate elements themselves, but most particularly to the relationship between them. Additional, perhaps more significant, meaning than either of the components contained individually, is implied.

This is described as a *dialectical* process, which means a fruitful collision of opposites (a

---

How? and What?

Juxtaposition deals with the storytelling method itself rather than addressing the content (the what? of the play). It responds to the basic question how? But as we saw in Chapter 2, the relationship between stories and the storytelling method is mutually defining:

- the story that you're telling is dependent on the way you tell the story.
- the way you tell the story is dependent on the story that you're telling.

So the how? of juxtaposition profoundly affects the story content, too.

---

familiar set of terms, in light of Chapter 5.) However, it's productive to think of it here as a dialogue, a reciprocating conversation between the two juxtaposed elements: one speaks, the other replies. It helps to remind us that juxtaposition is a dynamic process, actively and continuously moving between the poles of the newly related elements.

This harks back to the issue of latent energy, considered in Chapter 2 in the context of assessing initial ideas for plays. To sustain a full-length play that lasts 1½–2 hours, the initial idea has to have plenty of latent energy. This will then be released and expressed by the creation of movement and conflict within the arc of action. But you also need a means of building and banking energy during the arc, or there is a risk that, just as the action rises to its climactic moments, only the last vestiges will still remain to power it. (Think of taking one huge breath and trying to keep talking right to the last gasp. The final couple of sentences are usually rather feeble!) The play's expended energy has to be consistently replenished because this fuels the audience's imaginative engagement; if the play's energy flags, so does the audience's, and they disengage.

What is required is a kind of capacitor, a 'battery' to store and increase the reserves of energy throughout the action, ready to deliver the peak at full power. The principle of juxtaposition provides the means.

Juxtaposition *banks* the energy of the story rather than expending it, because of its ability to generate an extra layer of meaning to the dramatic components. It 'adds value' by suggesting to us that there is more in them, to be discovered by considering them reciprocally rather than individually. (The extra element might be, for example, a hint of something hidden, or of a more profound truth. Or it might be a form of 'decoder key' that helps us to make sense of two components that would otherwise be incomprehensible.) But note that juxtaposition brings nothing material to the equation: it's a catalyst. It has no innate reservoir of meaning itself. It is simply a method of organising the existing elements, creating stimulating alterations in our perceptions of them.

WHAT CAN BE JUXTAPOSED TO CREATE ENERGY?

Before returning to *Top Girls* to examine the principle at work, we should consider which dramatic components are available for juxtaposition.

EXERCISE
What are the 'building blocks' you, as playwright, have at your disposal to create interactive relationships suggestive of meaning? Try to think in terms of basic elements that are available for use in any play, whatever its particular subject matter or form.

COMMENTS
The following basic elements offer raw material to be juxtaposed, though they may be used very differently by individual playwrights:

Characters – Protagonist and antagonist, ally and opponent, for example. Audiences relate to characters through comparison and contrast with each other. (Who?)

Character and environment – The story world functions as a mirror that reflects character. The physical setting embodies the values, attitudes, desires, fears that motivate the character and the play's action. It is the character's specific context that can match him exactly, or contradict him. (Who? and where?)

Space – Movement within three related planes, and also the contrast between high and low status has been discussed. In Chapter 1, the spatial arrangements of the stage and auditorium offered a physical correlative to the feeling of proximity or distance you wish to create between your audience and the play. These are all juxtaposed spatial relationships. But in structuring the space of the story world itself, you can juxtapose interiors with exteriors (a dining room v. a road); private space with public space (your bathroom v. a swimming pool); expansive space (a field, the galaxy) v. contracted space (a prison cell, an aircraft).

Physical space v. imaginary space is the basic juxtaposition of theatre itself: the physical space of the stage juxtaposed with the imaginary space of the story world, which might be Rome, or the prairie or Mag and Maureen's kitchen. Within the story world, you can contrast a character's actual presence in a room with also being in a dream, hallucination or reverie. In *Hamlet*, when the Prince speaks in soliloquy, he is physically present in the Elsinore court, but this is set against his own private thoughts: another version of exterior v. interior, as well as physical v. imaginary space.

There is always a fruitful tension between onstage and offstage space that can be exploited to considerable effect: think about the use Martin McDonagh makes of these as Mag burns the party invitation in the nick of time before Maureen returns from feeding the chickens, or in the way 'offstage' represents, to Maureen, the alluring world beyond the claustrophobic kitchen. (Where?)

Time – Causal sequences are juxtaposed units of time. Effect follows cause in a forward progression that we term 'linear'. Stories can be structured in this linear form (the familiar beginning/middle/end pattern), but don't have to be. You can disrupt the forward movement of time in a variety of ways: flashbacks (to past events) or flashforwards (to future events) can be juxtaposed with events in the present. Many plays involving detection or investigation are structured in this way. You can run events simultaneously; this might be staged as a sequence, or could be placed side by side in the same physical space. For example, in Shakespeare's *Richard III*, the climactic Battle of Bosworth places the camps of King Richard and his opponent Richmond side by side on stage; the scene moves back and forth between the two leaders' tents as they dream about the next day's battle. This is a splendid example of juxtaposed story time *and* space: the space is both actual (Bosworth Field) and imaginary (the men's dreams).

The linear progression of time can be substituted by a circular pattern that returns to the beginning again in the final moments. Samuel Beckett does this in *Waiting for Godot*, where the two tramps, Vladimir and Estragon, finish in exactly the same state as they began: not going anywhere! You can juxtapose two or more historical time periods interwoven throughout the play: Mark Ravenhill's *Mother Clap's Molly House* moves back and forth between the eighteenth and twenty-first centuries, for example. (When?)

Language and physical activity – Spoken dialogue can be juxtaposed with accom-

Subtext: Writing 'between the Lines'

'Subtext' implies an additional dimension hidden beneath the surface of a character's speech or physical actions. It's the inner life of a word, a sentence or a gesture itself. The audience becomes aware of discrepancies between what a character says and the way she says it; between what she says and her subsequent course of action; between what she says and her facial expressions and body language as she says it. It can be inferred from silence, and from stillness, where we would otherwise expect speech and movement.

Subtext is motivated by the character's inner life, which you must know in detail. Sometimes, circumstances press him to disguise it, for reasons of deceit, self-preservation, or the thrill of possessing an illicit secret. You must know his reasons, but must also understand his need to 'give himself away'; for if he succeeds in hiding it, there will be no discrepancies, no hints – no subtext: only a calm, unruffled surface.

Explore conflict between the character's interior and exterior to locate points of friction and rupture in that smooth surface. Gradually reveal the hidden information through implication and inference, by creating a sustained system of counterpoints between language and physical activity.

panying gesture and movement, or with silence. Within dialogue, different types of speech can be juxtaposed. Within movement, different rhythms, pace, gestures, and stillness can be juxtaposed. These are ways in which the depth of a character is revealed; the audience draws from them the sense of an inner life, through subtext. (Who? what? why?)

Visual and aural elements – Dialogue is naturally the major component of the aural element of the play. But as The Visual and Aural Toolkit showed in Chapter 2, there are other, non-verbal kinds of sound that can be juxtaposed with dialogue. In both verbal and non-verbal sounds, tone, pitch, rhythm, pace and duration all carry significance. In the visual elements of gesture and movement, rhythm, pace and duration are significant, whilst colour, shape and texture are important in set, costume, lighting and properties.

Juxtapositions between visual and aural elements can produce complementary or contradictory outcomes. (What? and how?)

From this list, it's clear that every major component of a play can be harnessed into a form of relationship capable of generating the extra energy required.

TOP GIRLS

Caryl Churchill employs each of these elements to great effect in *Top Girls*. Marlene – the contemporary character in Act One – is the protagonist. The other five women are placed in relation to her, creating a series of points of view of Marlene for the audience. But they are also juxtaposed with each other in the same mutually informative way, so there is a multidimensional frame of reference at work.

The women are drawn from different time periods. Marlene is from 1982, Joan from the ninth century, Isabella from the nineteenth, while Nijo, Griselda and Gret hail from different periods of the Middle Ages: a juxtaposition of time. Each woman derives from a completely different geographic origin and brings with her a wealth of cultural contrast that is visually embodied in her physical appearance: a juxtaposition of space. Each also has her own distinct speech patterns and verbal idiom that is completely consonant with her appearance. So here, in the juxtaposition between the visual and the verbal, there is complementarity rather than contradiction. What Churchill is doing is contextualizing Marlene historically and culturally: we are being invited to view a contemporary woman in very deep perspective.

The women's conversation topics cover a broad range, but circle around one constant theme: the freedom or circumscription of a woman's identity and self-determination. This is explored through their relationships with men in the realm of love, sex and marriage; their experiences of childbirth and parenthood; their status within relationships of social, political and economic power. The issue of freedom or restriction is crystallized most strongly through the metaphor of travel: each of the six women has taken or is taking a literal or a figurative form of journey. The language, despite its variety of individual idioms, shares amongst all of the women an absolute exhilaration in their mobility, often precisely because it was forbidden or unexpected for them – as women – to be so.

And yet, whilst the language ranges widely across countries, up and down mountains, even (in the case of Gret) into the mouth of Hell itself, visually we are looking at a group of women seated around a dinner table. Apart from their individual entrances, a quick trip to the restroom by Marlene and the comings and goings of the Waitress, the physical action is static. So Churchill is employing another series of striking juxtapositions: visual v. verbal, movement v. stillness.

We're reminded, too, when we look at the women, that not only do they derive from different time periods, they are also not all historical figures. Isabella and Nijo are, but Gret is actually Dulle Griet, a figure from a famous Dutch painting in which she leads a mothers' army fighting hellish demons. Griselda, on the other hand, only exists in language: she is the subject of a fable, told variously by three different European poets. Her full title is 'Patient Griselda', famous for her submissive acquiescence to her husband, Walter. She was a peasant girl who married a nobleman in true fairytale fashion. He felt compelled to test her loyalty and obedience repeatedly, taking away each of her two children, and then seeming to abandon her for another wife. She accepted each act without complaint, and was eventually rewarded by the restoration of both her children and her position. Joan is the most intriguing of all: she may or may not be a historical figure, for her very existence was disputed by the Catholic Church. She describes herself very wittily: 'I'm a heresy myself.'

So the 'contextualizing' women are not only drawn from history but also from art and literature; that is, from different sites of representation. This juxtaposition raises a question: how are we to understand Marlene? She is not a historical figure. She exists only as a theatrical character, and is thus as fictionalized as Gret and Griselda. But is she (like Joan) a truth or a heresy? Does she embody a truth about contemporary women, or not?

Churchill accumulates energy at every point of comparison and contrast: parallel and echo, counterpoint and copy, deliver a matrix of meanings. But this is only the first Act of the play (in some published versions, Churchill's text is divided differently, and the dinner party sequence is the first scene). It is a *tour de force* in its own right, but in terms of the play's overall structure, it is actually a form of opening balance: a point of departure for the overall action.

Pause here and consider this question. It's completely unlike the kinds of opening balance studied in Chapter 4. Where within this Act, do you think, is the element of ongoing story that could deliver the play's subsequent action?

It has to be Marlene – she is the protagonist. So the overall arc of action tracks her. The story event of the scene (the answer to what?) is a celebratory dinner in Marlene's honour. As it progresses, the occasion of celebration is revealed: Marlene has been promoted to the position of Managing Director of an employment agency. She has become a 'Top Girl'.

So despite its unique form, the Act does still function as an opening balance: it sets up the story world of the protagonist, and the initial situation. But it has given us a breadth and depth of perspective on Marlene's story that is almost mythological in scope: it's a distancing technique that makes us literally stand back from her story and view it always in juxtaposition with other women in history and art.

ACTS TWO AND THREE

EXERCISE
In terms of patterns of structure explored earlier, how do you expect Marlene's story to continue to develop?

- What do you think might provide a form of disruption, to tip the story into motion?
- Do you expect the six women in Act One to reappear in Acts Two and Three?
- Do you think there will have to be other characters? If so, who might they be? In terms of character function?

- Where do you think there might be an opportunity to create conflict?

COMMENTS
- If Marlene's story begins with her promotion, then it must continue to explore her work situation. There has to be movement from the restaurant to the offices of her company. Act One situated Marlene within a broad context; now it's time for the focus to narrow down to show her own personal context. Following the hints in Act One, (the women's conversation topics) it's clear that the story will contrast Marlene's different roles as high-status working woman and her personal life, possibly as a wife and mother. Her relationships with men and with other women will have to be developed.

Since the opening balance establishes Marlene as the new boss (of the Top Girls Employment Agency), then it's possible that the disruptive element could be a threat to her job. She would have to respond by defending her position, and would end the play in success or defeat. The threat could originate from within her work situation, or from within her domestic life. That would be the likely pattern if the play is structured as a causal transformation.

- It would be highly unusual to create five such rich and striking characters in Act One only to abandon them completely in Acts Two and Three. So it's logical to expect that they will recur.

If the focus of the story shifts to the Employment Agency, there will have to be other characters who work there, and characters who are their clients. But also, if Marlene's domestic life is to be part of the story, there will need to be characters from this world, too: perhaps a husband or partner, and a child or two. Certainly, in a story that is so strongly about women's relationships with men, we could expect some male characters, for comparison and contrast. In which case, where and how will the five dinner party guests (a Catholic heresy, an oil painting, a poem and two long-dead historical figures!) be integrated into the continuing story? In terms of character function, the antagonist has yet to appear, and the allies and opponents need to be clarified.

- If the disruption centres upon a possible threat to Marlene's job, then there is a clear opportunity for conflict there. It may be conflict between her private and public worlds that constitutes the threat.

A substantial number of these speculations do, in fact, happen. Act Two switches to the Top Girls Agency, and new characters are introduced: Win and Nell are Marlene's junior associates in the company; Louise, Jeanine and Shona are all interviewees for jobs. Marlene's role as a high-powered business executive is indeed juxtaposed with her domestic life: although she isn't married, she does have a sister, Joyce, who is her exact opposite.

Joyce is a working-class divorcee living in Ipswich (their home town), bringing up Angie, a teenage girl of limited intelligence. The arc of action reveals that Marlene is actually Angie's mother. Angie doesn't know this; she believes Joyce is her mother, and idolizes her 'Aunty Marlene'. She does claim to suspect the true relationship, but this may just be a product of her idealization of her aunt. Marlene abandoned Angie as a baby, in order to escape her working-class origins and forge a career in London: a career that, as the play opens, has reached a new peak with her promotion.

This is an obvious site of past conflict, and it becomes so again in the play's climactic scene, a furious personal and political argument between Marlene and Joyce about freedom and responsibility. There is also a smaller, localized conflict at work, when Rosemary Kidd, wife of Marlene's defeated rival for the Managing Director's post, comes to ask Marlene to step down in favour of her husband. Howard Kidd is, she says, ill with the shock: 'What's it going to do to him working for a woman? I think if it was a man he'd get over it as something normal.'

However, there is no disruption of the kind studied previously, such as Pato Dooley's invitation to the party, or the Oracle's reply to Oedipus. There is no direct threat to Marlene's job. Churchill is not, in fact, employing a transformational structure driven by cause and effect logic. Her structure is based upon a series of juxtapositions.

CHARACTER VARIATIONS

Possibly the greatest surprise in *Top Girls* is that the five dinner guests in Act One never appear again. Or more specifically, they don't recur in that form. The speculation that the scope of the contextual frame created in Act One would probably narrow in Acts Two and Three to focus on Marlene, is correct. But Churchill doesn't want to abandon her method of advancing Marlene's story by placing her in a series of juxtaposed relationships with other women. In terms of distance/ proximity, she doesn't want us to lose our objective distance from Marlene and become sympathetic to her (because she is under threat and fighting to survive.) She wants us to retain a coolly critical stance towards her.

Instead of reprising the dinner party quintet, Churchill incorporates the comparative and contrasting energy they generated into a new series of women. These are now all contemporary characters. Each of them embodies some particular aspect of modern women's lives, attitudes and behaviour, but also echoes elements of the dinner guests. Rosemary Kidd, for example, incorporates aspects of Patient Griselda, in her wifely role at the mercy of her husband's whims and moods. Aspects of Gret, the stoical mother who is finally driven to action in retaliation for the killing of her children, are incorporated into Joyce. Marlene's sister resents the burden of caring for Angie thrust upon her by Marlene's abandonment. Joyce, we learn, suffered a miscarriage of her own baby due to stress: Angie is a difficult, sullen and demanding child. Yet she has shouldered the maternal role and fiercely defends her daughter, as Gret does her children.

There are contrasts, too, in these incorporations: for example, Nijo, the self-willed courtesan who declines to fade into obscurity after losing the Emperor's favour, is contrasted with Win, one of the recruiters at the Agency. Win is ostensibly an independent woman determined to carve out a career for herself; yet she is also the mistress of a married man, conversant with all the roses in his prize garden, compelled to hide in his car to avoid his neighbours seeing her arrive. Nijo, in contrast, though bound by the rigid conventions of Court etiquette, absolutely refuses to accept the Emperor's right to beat her. She colludes with the other Imperial concubines and gives him a taste of his own medicine.

Churchill ensures that the energy of these comparative incorporations deepens through-out the play, in the use of actors' 'doubling'. This is often a practical strategy employed by directors with a limited number of actors in production. Each actor plays more than one role, so they appear twice. If they play three roles, it's known as 'trebling'. Usually, the audience is expected to ignore the fact that they have seen the actor in a different role, and accept them anew. In *Top Girls* however, the pattern of role doubling and trebling is specified in the script, and the audience is invited to notice the actor's reappearance. We are challenged to contemplate the juxtaposition of roles each actor plays. In these ways, the breadth and depth of reference that Churchill created in Act One is maintained in Acts Two and Three: the perspective doesn't, in fact, shrink. It shifts ground.

Who Churchill leaves out is also surprising. There are no male characters in *Top Girls* – though they are endlessly the topic of conversation, men are conspicuous by their absence. It is Howard Kidd's wife who comes to challenge Marlene, not Howard himself. Men occupy the offstage space, whilst women occupy the onstage space; the men are brought onstage only through the women's conversation. Thus, the men are being described and interpreted by the women – represented by them, just as dinner guests Gret and Griselda were representations of women by male artists.

TIME, SPACE AND STORY

As predicted, Churchill does contrast Marlene's working life with her domestic life – but not in the expected way. We don't go to Marlene's home, nor do we have a sense of her private life running in parallel time with her work. Instead, the Top Girls Agency offices are juxtaposed spatially with Joyce's house and garden in Ipswich.

The first shift of space is from the Act One restaurant to the Agency in Act Two. We learn that the dinner party took place on Saturday night, and this is now the following Monday morning. So far, progression of time is linear, and the spatial shift is also logical in terms of story development. But the progress does not continue in linear and logical fashion. From the Agency offices on Monday morning, in the next scene we shift back in time to the previous afternoon (Sunday). This could be viewed as a form of flashback, but usually flashbacks

occur when we need to be given a crucial piece of story information. But is this the case here?

The scene takes place outside in Joyce's garden, in a makeshift shelter constructed by two completely new characters: Angie and her friend Kit. Gradually it becomes clear who Joyce and Angie are (Marlene's sister and 'niece'.) Angie's hostility towards Joyce causes her to make idle violent threats; her idolization of 'Aunty Marlene' prompts her to plan to run away to London to visit. These new characters and their world give us another, completely different perspective from which to view Marlene: a fresh juxtaposition. But they don't give us the kind of story development we're accustomed to: Angie's plan doesn't constitute the anticipated threat to Marlene's job. And at this point, although we have now been introduced to Angie (and Joyce), we don't know the true nature of Marlene's relationship to the child. We won't learn this until the end of the play.

From Ipswich, the scene reverts back to the Agency, and once more it's Monday morning. Now, just before Rosemary Kidd arrives, Angie turns up: she has carried out her previous day's plan of running away to visit Marlene. We could expect this to produce some important forward movement in the story, in the form of consequences: Marlene would have to deal with Angie's unexpected arrival. But it doesn't. The action of the scene shifts focus almost immediately from Marlene's awkwardness with Angie to what is, for her, much more familiar territory: doing battle with Mrs. Kidd. Angie, in fact, spends more time with Win than she does with Marlene.

The Agency scenes are further complicated by 'inset' sequences of interviews conducted by, respectively, Marlene, Nell and Win. These clearly take place at the offices on the Monday morning, but our sense of precise time and place is uncertain. Where and when are they in relation to the discussions between the

Agency staff? (For example, the first Agency scene consists *only* of an interview between Marlene and Jeanine, yet we don't see Marlene arrive at work until the second Agency scene.)

And there is one more structural surpise to come. We might expect the story development of Angie's arrival to produce some logical outcome: Joyce perhaps coming to collect her, or Marlene taking her back to Ipswich. Time would move forward again. But instead, Act Three is set on a Sunday evening *one year earlier.*

The setting is once again Joyce's house – in the kitchen this time, an interior as opposed to the earlier exterior scene. Marlene arrives to visit Joyce and Angie, bringing presents. It emerges that Angie had asked her to come, pretending it was Joyce's request. The two sisters are ranged against each other: first through Angie's different responses to them, and then, when Angie has gone off to bed, in a long head-to-head argument. Visually, the scene reverts to an echo of the dinner party: women sitting at a table, talking. But this time it is a kitchen table, and the range of comparison and contrast between multiple women is reduced to just two. It is in this scene that the play's scope finally narrows down to Marlene's story; but it is compression, not shrinkage. All of the play's earlier women are now compressed into these two sisters, related by blood but contrasted in every other way. The compression produces intensification, and we are finally brought into close proximity, as the row – fuelled by alcohol, as the dinner party was 'lubricated' by wine – reveals the truth about Marlene's history.

Why has the time shift occurred? In story terms, what has it given us? If we trace the pattern, the sequence is:

- Restaurant. Saturday night. Marlene and her guests celebrate her promotion with lashings of wine and food, and many personal stories.
- Employment Agency. Monday morning. Marlene interviews Jeanine.
- Joyce's garden. The previous afternoon (Sunday). Angie tells her friend Kit that she's going to kill Joyce with a brick, and that she's going to run off to London to visit her Aunty Marlene.
- Employment Agency. Monday morning. – Win and Nell discuss Marlene's promotion and their own prospects. – Marlene arrives, and is greeted with their applause. – Win interviews Louise. – Angie arrives. – Rosemary Kidd arrives, and argues with Marlene. – Marlene goes. – Nell interviews Shona. – Win and Nell talk to Angie. Angie falls asleep. – Marlene returns, with news that Howard Kidd has suffered a heart attack and been taken to hospital. She considers the sleeping Angie.
- Joyce's kitchen. Sunday afternoon, one year earlier. Marlene arrives with presents. Marlene and Joyce fight.

It's apparent that the bulk of the story takes place over approximately thirty-six hours – Saturday evening to Monday morning. The story begins with celebration of Marlene's promotion and moves forward to show her and her colleagues at work. Marlene's niece turns up to visit, a plan concocted in a flashback to the previous afternoon. But Angie's arrival doesn't deflect Marlene from her job: she carries on regardless, and we see why she has been preferred as Managing Director when she smartly dispatches her rival's complaining wife. Marlene clearly is a tough, smart and talented Top Girl.

A 'DOUBLE' ENDING

Act Three, with its large time shift, shows us something of the 'collateral damage' incurred along the path of Marlene's rise to success. To realize her own potential, she has shed every aspect of her private life: her working-class background, family and none-too-bright daughter. This ruthlessness has left them floundering in her wake. Marlene's attitude is hardheaded: 'the devil take the hindmost.' The end of the play, however, reveals that the 'hindmost' is Marlene's own child.

The time shift allows a remarkable form of double ending that throws Marlene once more into very deep perspective. Throughout, she has been viewed as if through a series of refracting lenses, created by the pattern of juxtapositions Churchill manufactures with the other women characters. It's an effect that could compare to a hall of mirrors: each time Marlene is reflected back, a different aspect of her is highlighted. In the end, she becomes the sum of her multiple reflections. Churchill delivers this final image in two (staggered) lines of dialogue that bridge the time shift.

After the long argument in Joyce's kitchen, Marlene, settling down to sleep on the sofa, is disturbed by Angie. The child is having a nightmare, and calls out for her Mum. It's the one moment when Marlene could acknowledge her child, but she doesn't. She asks Angie if she's had a bad dream: Angie's reply: 'Frightening.' This is the last word of the play, a disturbing place to end: the distressed and disoriented child, ill-equipped to cope with the world.

But if we unravel the time shift, this remark was actually made twelve months *before* Marlene's rise. If we go back to the previous scene, in the Agency where Angie turns up to visit her 'Aunty' and is once again discarded, we hear Marlene's judgement upon her daughter:

```
WIN. She's a nice kid. Isn't she?
MARLENE. She's a bit thick. She's a bit
funny.
```

```
WIN. She thinks you're wonderful.
MARLENE. She's not going to make it.
```

The 'double' ending resides in those two lines: one is the last line of the *story* ('She's not going to make it.'), the other is the last line of the *play*: 'Frightening.' This final juxtaposition gives us a last, summative reflection of Marlene.

WHO IS MARLENE'S ANTAGONIST?

There is one last question to consider, and that is the problem of an antagonist. Where would you locate this function? Certainly the play provides a series of allies – Nell and Win; the dinner party guests – and opponents – Rosemary Kidd; Joyce. But the pattern of juxtapositions throughout leaves us with only one possible candidate – Angie – and she seems the least equipped of all to oppose Marlene. Angie doesn't actively block Marlene's progress through the story, as the antagonist conventionally does. Instead, she is Marlene's buried past – her 'baggage'.

Angie's 'not going to make it', while Marlene conspicuously has. But at whose expense? In the Act One dinner party, each of the five guests describes an ambivalent attitude towards motherhood. Isabella found no room within her sense of 'mission' for children; she prefers horses. Joan, divesting herself of a woman's identity, failed to recognize the signs of pregnancy. Nijo gave birth to a number of children by different fathers. She discriminates between the relative value of boy and girl children ('It was only a girl but I was sorry to lose it.') Griselda's children were taken away from her for years by her husband, while some of Gret's ten children were horribly murdered by the Spanish invaders.

Marlene remains silent in Act One on the

subject of children. We could read her refusal to acknowledge Angie as simply cold-hearted. Her evaluation of Angie's prospects is certainly brutal. But it is also disturbingly accurate, given the aggressively ambitious contemporary world reflected by the Top Girls Agency. Careful examination of the dinner party guests reveals that their attitudes and experiences are the complex sum of their cultural and historical situations. Their losses and gains, their ambivalence towards partners and children, their griefs and joys, arise not simply from the strengths and weaknesses within their individual characters but from a series of often antagonistic contexts. Churchill's structure throughout requires us to view Marlene within the same interlocking mesh of contexts. The play's closing image that juxtaposes Marlene with Angie, ensures that the audience's sympathies remain alienated from the protagonist. In terms of function, this employs Angie in an antagonistic role. But if we recall the image/shadow method of creating protagonist and antagonist, then Angie should also be understood as Marlene's shadow form. Their final dialogue exchange thus takes on a deeper, more disturbing mutual resonance:

```
MARLENE. Did you have a bad dream? What
    happened in it? Well you're awake
    now, aren't you pet?
ANGIE. Frightening.
```

Top Girls' structure of discontinuous time, space, character and story is an extraordinarily powerful dramatic assembly. It accumulates energy at every turn by placing its components in dialectical relationships. In doing so, it achieves a depth of perspective on its protagonist that I have earlier described as 'mythological': though Marlene is historically specific to the time of writing (1982), she has lost little of her resonance 20 years on.

Churchill has rendered her an iconic figure, through the principle of juxtaposition.

SCRIPT EXERCISE

The brief for this exercise isn't as complex as *Top Girls*! It does, however, require you to think about different points of view, and about developing your story through juxtaposition.

As in the conflict script exercise, allow plenty of time to develop the characters and the story outline before progressing to writing the script itself. This exercise, especially, needs quite a bit of forethought.

It's going to be the longest of the exercises so far, because it will require you to write a series of small scenes. Aim for three or four scenes. Don't make them too long, at least for the first attempt: keep the overall script length to about twelve pages.

Choose one of the following scenarios:

• Two brothers are attending their only sister's funeral. Each man has to give a short memorial address to the congregation, describing the sister. Each man's memory of her is rather different. Which picture is the true one: one of the brothers' versions, or another altogether?
• At an auction preview, a woman opens an antique wooden chest. It contains an old banknote, a woman's hairbrush, two ancient railway tickets and fragments of a torn letter. She is intrigued: who owned them, and what is the story behind them?
• A new young army recruit sits on the bus taking him to basic training camp. What will the next few months hold in store for him? Will he be a good soldier? Or will enlisting have been a disastrous mistake?

If these three scenarios don't inspire you, there are alternative sources you can use for ideas.

Exercise Checklist

- Remember that the best stories are rooted in character. Ensure that each new detail you show us develops our knowledge of them. Think especially about how each action, each situation, helps this.
- Use comparison and contrast between characters to deepen our understanding.
- Use the list of elements that can be juxtaposed to stimulate your thinking.
- Don't allow yourself to become bogged down in technique at the expense of telling a good story.
- Try not to spell everything out for us: use the juxtapositions to reveal information in more subtle ways.

Collect a series of very different images from newspapers and magazines, and lay them out in as many varying patterns as you can find. What thoughts strike you? Or you could choose a familiar object from your home and dramatise its history. Or simply go and sit quietly in a corner of a coffee shop and observe the other customers: develop and interweave the stories of at least two of them.

Ask your reader to give you feedback on the script, as usual. You want to know whether they understood the story clearly; ask them to tell you which were the key points. Ask them to give you a short description of each of your characters: did they pick up the details you wanted them to find? Did they intepret them as you expected?

COMMENTS
Review the scene yourself in light of the reader's comments.

Identify which elements performed their task well, and which didn't. Try to determine why the unsuccessful elements failed to deliver your expectations.

- Did you become too obscure in some of the links you hoped to make?
- Did the attempt to juxtapose characters render them a bit less human, rather mechanical? Perhaps you didn't develop the character profiles alongside one another, to identify where they echoed or counterpointed each other. Or perhaps you tried to compare and contrast too many elements in an exercise of only twelve pages.
- Did your reader lose track of where and when things were happening in the story? Perhaps there were too many shifts of time and space, or possibly the transitions between different time periods or locations weren't signalled clearly enough. Go back to the list of elements which can be juxtaposed: did you exploit, for example, the

Five Key Characteristics

To help create comparison and contrast within a character, and between characters, it's useful to identify five key personal characteristics.

- Rank them in hierarchical order. Which is the dominant characteristic (number one)?
- Examine the other four. How does the dominant one provoke or modify each of the others? Once you are clear about this internal form of juxtaposition, set the individual (ranked) lists for each character alongside each other, and look at how the lists interact.

different kinds of sound, or visual elements, to help make the transitions clear?

- Were the time/space shifts necessary in order to reveal information?
- Did you find yourself avoiding time/space shifts and instead have your characters supply information through rather clumsy expositional speeches? Exposition is essential information that the audience needs to know, but it needs to be delivered subtly, or it can seem as though your characters have suddenly forgotten vital information and have to be reminded ('You're my brother, you say? And our only sister has just died? That's upsetting.') But you may simply have been nervous about controlling the shifts; if so, try just one simple flashback to get you started.
- Juxtaposition should help to change the audience's point of view of the characters and the story. Did the juxtapositions you selected actually do this? If not, perhaps you need to think about what is new information, or a new light thrown on existing information, that the juxtaposition

should have disclosed. It should add an extra layer of meaning.

Remember the watchwords of the conflict script exercise: the hallmarks of your own distinctive writer's voice.

- Simplicity
- Economy
- Clarity
- Meaning
- Feeling

Use your notes and evaluations to rewrite the draft. Rework it and resubmit it to your reader until you're satisfied that it achieves your aims successfully. But in doing so, don't lose the freshness of your original idea: if the energy – the *life* – of the scene is clear to the audience, they will forgive some roughness of technique. If, on the other hand, the technique is wonderful but the vivacity of the idea has seeped away, the audience won't engage. So a valuable lesson to learn is when to stop rewriting.

7 WRITING THE SCRIPT: DIALOGUE AND STAGE DIRECTIONS

ISSUING INVITATIONS

In the preceding chapters, we've considered the relationship between yourself, as playwright, the raw material of your play, and the audience with whom you wish to communicate. The main focus of study has been the underlying structure of dramatic storytelling, and we've also thought about the physical means that will deliver the play in performance: the visual and aural systems.

Now our attention turns to the first group of people with whom you will collaborate: the director, actors and designers, who will translate your play into the four dimensions of space and time in production. These are the people who will help you finally reach your audience. So it's vitally important, in writing your script, to make sure that your intended communication is as clearly and precisely expressed in the dialogue and stage directions as it can be, to minimize the opportunity for misinterpretation. These elements are the means by which your individual writer's voice is heard: they must, therefore, carry the ring of your true note.

In an ideal situation, a new play would be developed through workshops with a director and actors during your writing process, so that you could see and hear your scenes up on their feet. This would allow you to refine the structure, enrich the characters and polish the dialogue and stage directions through rewrites with the help of their constant input. Often, for practical reasons of money and time, the workshop and production rehearsal periods are combined; again, it's valuable for the playwright, if possible, to be present throughout to share and receive feedback.

But just as it is important for your script to express your intentions with clarity, economy and simplicity, it's equally vital that it should excite the creative imagination of the production team. Each member of the team has a different field of focus: each actor is searching for a way to connect with her character; the designers are looking at how the story world is evoked; the director wants to see the overarching structure of the story, to understand how best to guide the team towards realizing your play. Each member brings to your script his own set of questions; and just as we've noted throughout that the specific nature of your questions, as writer, will be personally indicative of you, so too will the actor's, director's and designer's questions be personal to him or her. Your script must therefore extend a personal invitation to each member of the team to enter into the imaginative arena; and it must give them sufficient room to operate within it.

The first, and most basic, consideration is how to lay out the script on the page so

A Great Party

I have been told that the art of directing is akin to throwing a great party. It means creating an atmosphere of freedom and security in which the participants feel relaxed enough to let rip and sufficiently confident to go a little beyond their everyday boundaries. It's a warm and receptive shared environment where that little bit of inventive personal daring is met with other people's delight, and is matched. The same thing is true of the art of stage writing: your aim should be to challenge and excite the production team with your characters, the story and the way you are telling it, to take them beyond their usual limits and invite them to pitch in. You should aim to write a great party.

that it's immediately accessible. Don't forget that it will first be read when it is received by a production company; it should, therefore, be *readable*.

A READABLE SCRIPT LAYOUT

- Scripts should be typed or word-processed. Handwritten scripts won't be read, professionally; and from your point of view, it's hard to assess the script's running time in handwritten form. You can buy scriptwriting software, but it's not necessary; it's easy enough to create your own page templates with a basic word-processing package. If you don't have access to a computer, you can handwrite initially, but have the script typed and properly formatted for submission.
- Standard page size is A4, printed on one side of the paper only. This isn't wasteful; the reverse side of the page is used for notes in workshop and rehearsal by the production personnel. Staging and technical cues are always written here for performance.
- All pages should be numbered, for ease of reference.
- Also for the purposes of notes, there should be decent margins at the sides, head and foot of the page. Allow an inch and a half side margins, and a minimum of two inches at either end.
- Character names as speech indicators should be kept to the left margin. Stage directions usually begin at the left margin, and use the whole width of the page (though where they occur within the course of a speech, they can be idented.) It's helpful always to use capital letters for characters' names in stage directions and speech indicators; in dialogue, however, where another character refers to someone by name, this should be in lower case after the initial capital letter.
- In published editions of plays, dialogue often slightly overlaps the character name. (In Chapter 6, my quotations from *Top Girls* show this.) It's clearer, though, when the two are kept separate; if you create an internal margin at which every line of dialogue begins, the reader can immediately see where speeches begin and end, and who is speaking at any given moment.
- Use double spacing between complete speeches, or between speeches and stage directions. Within a speech or a stage direction, single spacing is fine. The reader can tell at a glance where dialogue is advancing in short exchanges or in extended speeches, and can assess their rhythm and pace visually. This spacing also allows the running time to be estimated:

one page of A4 roughly equates to one minute, depending upon the pace and the nature of the action.

- Use a simple font such as Courier New or Times New Roman, in twelve-point pitch size (anything smaller is hard to read; larger is a waste of paper, and makes running time difficult to assess.) It's not essential to switch to italics or to capitals for stage directions, as published plays do – proper use of line spacing is clear enough. But if you are happier doing this, it's fine (though time-consuming); once you have established a convention for this, use it consistently throughout the script. Dialogue is always in lower case, with capitals used only for the beginning of sentences and proper names.

- Try to avoid falling into the habit of regularly underlining or italicizing dialogue. Actors don't appreciate being repeatedly told how to say lines. It may be necessary however where you want them to play against the obvious sense of the line – using irony, or indicating subtext, for example. (But if the dialogue continually requires additional emphatic signalling, it may be that the line isn't quite good enough. Improve the line!) It is useful to embolden Act and Scene indicators to make the structure clear (you might, alternatively, divide your play into Part One and Two around an interval).

Fig. 13 shows a sample page layout you might like to use.

SCENE TWO: Maria Before The Fair

MARIA and her sister ANN in the MARTENS' cottage. ANN is sweeping the floor. MARIA sprawls, a gardening apron over her dress.

MARIA   I was right about that old rosebush, Ann. 'Tweren't barren after all, just needed shifting. Fresh-turned soil and a clear look at the sunshine, and see, now it's blossoming. The buds are almost open, and as fat as ripe cherries. A pretty sight they'll turn out to be, a garden full of crimson.

ANN   Well, you've green fingers. Everyone says it.

MARIA   (with a shrug) P'rhaps it's fellow-feeling.
(ANN looks a question) Some of us might be refreshed by an hour or two in the sun.

ANN   But you spend all day out, tending the plants. Not like me, cooped up in here, shuffling dust into corners. You get all the sun that's going.

MARIA   Aye. But it's still Polstead sun. On Polstead soil.
(She shakes her head)
You almost done, Mistress Floorsweeper?

ANN   Reckon.

MARIA licks her finger, draws it across the floor and inspects it solemnly.

MARIA   Reckon not.

Figure 13   Sample script layout.

THINKING ABOUT DIALOGUE

Stage dialogue is not the same thing as everyday conversational speech. In realistic contemporary plays, it may appear to be so, but this is a carefully constructed illusion. In fact, realistic dialogue is as complex and artificial a construction as Shakespearean blank verse. Dialogue has a series of tasks to perform and goals to achieve within the structure of storytelling. Unlike everyday conversation, it cannot ramble or become sidetracked into incomprehensible blind alleys; it must be immediately clear. Where its meaning is intended to be ambiguous, it shouldn't be confusing: writing ambiguity means indicating clearly the range of possible meanings it could hold. It should be as economical as possible, making every word earn its presence; this is as true of Lucky's monologue in Beckett's *Waiting for Godot* – an explosive, garbled tumult of linguistic excess – as it is of Linda Loman's succinct exhortation over her husband Willy's grave, in Arthur Miller's *Death of A Salesman*: 'Attention must be paid.'

THE FUNCTION OF DRAMATIC DIALOGUE

Dramatic dialogue performs key functions:

Exposition: the revelation of specific information that the audience needs to know for the purposes of story development. It may concern the location and nature of the story world (when? and where?); important information about characters in terms of background or relationships (who?); and it will involve a statement of the opening balance (what?).

Character development: what a character says and the particular way in which he says it reveals him to us. He should have his own individual speech patterns and idioms: his own 'voice'. This will involve, for example, his vocabulary, rhythms of speech, the structure of his sentences, patterns of repetition and omission, whether he addresses a topic directly or obliquely. (You should be able to cover up the speech indicator on the page and still be able to determine which character is speaking, because of its distinctiveness.) From his dialogue, we should be able to glean his underlying motivation through the juxtaposition with his physical actions, and be able to predict his subsequent behaviour (who? why? what?).

Story development: what characters say, and when and how, moves the story foward. Here, dialogue is the vehicle for action. In *The Beauty Queen of Leenane*, for example, Maureen's last act of catastrophic violence is provoked by a slip of Mag's tongue which gives away the fact that she has burned a second invitation from Pato Dooley.

Description: theatre is an imaginative realm that works through compressed and intensified metaphors. Description – of people, places, things, feelings – is a means of expanding the dramatic metaphors. It can be used to create atmosphere and tone in scene-setting, as in Shakespeare's *Macbeth*, where Banquo and Duncan describe Macbeth's castle:

```
DUNCAN    This castle hath a pleasant
              seat; the air
          Nimbly and sweetly
              recommends itself
          Unto our gentle senses.
BANQUO    This guest of summer
          The temple-haunting
              martlet, does approve
          By his lov'd mansionry that
              the heaven's breath
          Smells wooingly here:
```

It can also provide moments of rest within the forward momentum of the story, time for the audience to catch up and reflect.

Commentary: this may be used to provide perspective on character and story development, as a form of criticism or evaluation. It sets events and people within a broader context, providing a framework of comparison and contrast. In Greek drama, this was a significant function of the Chorus. In contemporary drama, it's often the province of an individual character who may be acting as a narrator, on a temporary basis. It will, in these cases, sometimes be written as a monologue addressed directly to the audience.

'Dialogue' itself specifically means a conversation between characters. Usually, the conversation doesn't acknowledge the existence of the audience, and doesn't specifically address them. If a character wishes to signal awareness of their presence, and to address them during the course of a conversation with another character, this minor, peripheral, dialogue is called an 'aside'. You would indicate this to the actor by placing the stage direction '(aside)' directly before the line that is to be addressed to the audience. Conventionally, only the audience is understood to hear the aside; other characters don't hear it.

Characters can, however, talk directly and extensively to the audience; this is known as 'direct address'. It's usually a one-sided conversation, as there is no expectation that the audience will answer. It therefore becomes a monologue. Where the character is alone, does not acknowledge the audience and talks instead to herself, this is a 'soliloquy' or 'interior monologue'. It should be clear from the context and the content whether the speech is directed outwardly or inwardly; no specific stage direction is needed.

It's important to think about questions of address and awareness – levels of consciousness – when you are writing dialogue. Think about to whom the character is actually speaking. (Of course, the audience hears all the dialogue, but they are not always being directly addressed.) A character's awareness of the audience's presence is, similarly, distinct from the actor's awareness

Telling v. Showing

Writing a good play is not simply a question of writing long speeches. Drama means 'something that is done'; writing a play means *making things happen*, in front of us. Dramatic dialogue is a form of action, and, like other forms, it has purpose and direction. Its purpose is to tell us information, but because theatre is a visual medium, 'telling' must occur within a larger framework of 'showing'.

'Showing' requires you to think always about what is being done, in terms of the story. What is happening now? Why is this character speaking? What is his goal in saying this? And there will be as many times when you communicate this to us without speech, through the visual and non-verbal aural systems. But your primary form of 'showing' will be through the structure of the storytelling itself – through the interplay between movement, action, conflict and juxtaposition – and through the style of the play. So 'storytelling', a term we've inherited from the oral tradition, in theatre is really 'story showing', too.

(that is, naturally, constant.) The degree (or lack) of awareness, and the extent of the character's self-absorption, are aspects of character (who?) and style (how?)

THE ACT OF SPEAKING

Dramatic characters always speak for a reason; where they don't have one, they shouldn't speak. When you're writing dialogue, find the reason. Ask:

- What is the particular nature of the exchange – the transaction – between the characters at this point? Is it, for example, an argument, an invitation, a declaration, an interrogation, a proposal? What, in other words, are these characters doing? (What?)
- Why is this transaction happening at this point in the story action? How has it been motivated by what has just happened, or happened earlier? How will it motivate what will happen next? (Why?)
- What does the speaker want to achieve with this speech? Specifically, what does she want the other character to do in response? (Why?)

RHYTHM, WEIGHT AND MELODY

Writing good dialogue is very much like writing music; it requires you to cultivate an ear for rhythm and cadence, for the melody and weight of a line. By rhythm and cadence, I mean the rise and fall, the flow of a line; the cadence is its pulse. Melody and weight refer to the character's thoughts and feelings as expressed by the full shape of the line. In the example from *Macbeth*, above, try reading aloud Duncan's lines, that are one complete sentence. The thought is that the castle is beautiful and welcoming; Duncan feels

Actioning

To help you work out what the speaker wants from the listener, put yourself in the character's place, and choose a transitive verb that describes his goal. Make the verb specific to the action: rather than simply 'tell', does the character 'inform' or does he 'command'? A transitive verb is one that has a direct object: express it as 'I command you', 'I invite you', 'I insult you.' Rather than saying 'I propose marriage to you', which opens up a little too much distance between the speaker and the addressee, express it as 'I ask you to marry me.' And avoid saying 'I am asking you to marry me'; this formulation talks about you, rather than what you are doing to the other person. If you give the character a goal and an action that will achieve it when you plan the speech, writing will mean, first and foremost, making the speech carry out the action.

It also helps you to set up the continuation of the dialogue: the other character responds to what has just been done to them by accepting it or by rejecting it. 'I command you' could be met by a reciprocal 'I obey you' or 'I refuse you', that would develop the sequence along two quite different courses.

relaxed, looking forward to being a guest there. So the rhythm is unhurried, takes time to pause over the descriptive 'pleasant', 'nimbly' and 'sweetly'. Then the sentence pivots around the verb 'recommends itself' to propel it towards completion. You can hear the weight of completion in 'gentle senses'. I interrupted Banquo's speech, which is a very long sentence, at a punctuation break; if you read it aloud, you might be able to hear that, although it breaks well enough for sense and rhythm at the point of interruption, the underlying thought isn't yet completed, and so the weight of 'smells wooingly here' isn't quite right.

Thinking about the structure of each line of dialogue as you write – about length, word order, vocabulary and punctuation – is helped immensely if you remember always that dialogue is written *to be spoken aloud*. It is written for the human voice, and for the ear, not for the eye. What you write on the page will emerge on the actor's breath, beginning in the centre of his body, resonating through his chest, head and facial bones, and then shaped by his mouth. Stage dialogue is not 'words on a page', it is a physical entity. So when you write, write for the actor's mouth; keep trying your dialogue aloud, to hear how it sounds. Stage dialogue should feel good to speak, and *taste* good!

Punctuation tells the actor which point in the arc of a complete thought you have reached, and helps her direct her energy. It helps to excavate the meaning of the sentence. A full stop is a thought completed. An exclamation mark is a completion, but ends upon rising energy. A question mark also ends on rising energy, but is incomplete – it is completed by the actor who answers. A comma is a moment of rest, with the thought still continuing. So too are colons and semi-colons; they signal changes of direction in the thought, and invite a different calibre of energy from the actor to deliver this. A dash is an interrupted thought, whilst a '...' ending implies that the thought has trailed away into silence.

Some playwrights, such as Harold Pinter and Samuel Beckett, are meticulous about punctuation, and about the placing and

Overlapping Dialogue

Traditionally, stage dialogue takes the form of speeches in an alternating sequence, with characters speaking in turn. This is the way speeches appear on the page, one after another. But in real life, people rarely speak in strict sequence. We tend to interrupt and overlap each other, sometimes talking simultaneously; this is particularly so in families or close-knit groups who know each other well, or where heated emotions are in play. Caryl Churchill pioneered a means of notating overlapping speech on the page, to try to capture this realistic weave. She uses it in *Top Girls*.

Speeches are still laid out in sequence, but where a second character begins to speak before her predecessor has finished, a backward slash

(/) is inserted at the point of interruption. This cues the second actor to begin speaking. Sometimes the interruption will continue throughout the speech; in this case, the continuation is written as the next speech in the sequence, but doesn't begin with a capital letter (to indicate that the thought is still continuing.)

It is a wonderful technique to hear in performance, but very difficult to control in writing, and hard to decipher on the page. If you would like the actors to overlap the speeches to an extent but don't feel confident about fully writing the overlaps, you can simply indicate this with a stage direction, and they will experiment with the timing:

```
ANN (overlapping)      But you spend all day out, tending the plants. Not like
                       me, cooped up in here, shuffling dust into corners. You
                       get all the sun that's going.
MARIA (overlapping)    Aye. But it's still Polstead sun. On Polstead soil.
```

timing of pauses and silence. Others are not, and elect to leave their dialogue relatively unpunctuated, trusting the actor to find her own phrasing, emphasis and breathing points from the shape of the sentence itself. It's up to you which works best for your own writing. It's better to err on the side of under-writing punctuation rather than over-writing; the actor will find what feels right, and is consonant with sense.

Whilst these comments are fresh in your mind, it would be useful to go back and review your dialogue in each of your earlier script exercises, and to improve it.

THINKING ABOUT STAGE DIRECTIONS

Stage directions are everything in a script that isn't dialogue. They are the primary carriers of the visual system and of the non-verbal elements of the aural system, but they can additionally be used to modify or qualify dialogue. They are also a significant repository for your own voice as a writer, in the way you choose to write them: your choice of vocabulary, tone and selection of detail.

The audience never hears or sees your stage directions; they are mediated and interpreted by the production team. So the basic function of a stage direction is to give an instruction to a member of the team. But while they are instructions, don't think of them as orders. Stage directions are one of the most valuable means of stimulating the actor's, director's and designer's creative imagination, so try to think of them as invitations. Use them to call into play the special skills of the person to whom they are addressed.

Stage directions are often the area of a script most subject to interpretation by the production team; much more so than dialogue, they are shared territory. For this reason, it's worth understanding how to use

them to stimulate and to free the team, rather than to constrain them.

THE FUNCTION OF STAGE DIRECTIONS

Stage directions fulfil a number of key functions:

Scene setting: a description of the story world that may involve stipulating specific items of the physical set and their spatial organisation, is often the first information that appears in a scene. Some nineteenth- and twentieth-century playwrights were very detailed in their requirements, but contemporary writers tend to be briefer and less prescriptive. A good way to approach this is to think in terms of the dramatic metaphor: what might be the key visual or aural indicators of it? Try to convey the atmosphere and tone of the story world. (Where? When?)

Scene structure: stage directions indicate the beginnings and endings of scenes. At the most basic level, this could be via scene headings: Scene One, Scene Two, or via characters' entrances and exits. More important is their orchestration of the rhythm and tempo of a scene, shaping and directing its energy expenditure. Because stage directions are a major vehicle for 'showing', they work in counterpoint to the 'telling' of the dialogue. They indicate where a visual or sound effect punctuates the flow of speeches; where movement and gesture underscore or contradict dialogue; and where silence and stillness might occur. Through their control of timing, they help to sculpt the shape of the scene. (When? What? How?)

Character: these can be indications of key aspects of the character, of his physical appearance or personality. They can prompt the actor as to his state of mind or emotional condition. This is best achieved by considering how that might be shown, through gesture and movement. What does the character do at this point? How does that reveal his internal processes, his inner life? In particular, if you are writing subtext, think about the juxtaposition between his speech and his body language, or in the relative timing of speech, silence, movement and stillness. Think about the precise placing of the stage direction, to reveal information by controlling rhythm and tempo. They can also be used as hints in dialogue, where the actor may be required to play against the obvious sense of the line, or to punctuate the words with non-verbal utterances such as cries, screams or coughs. (Who? Why? What? How?)

Each of these functions needs to be handled with considerable care. It is better to err on the side of omission rather than inclusion: Greek drama contained no stage directions at all, and many contemporary plays employ very few.

What is at stake here is the question of freeing and stimulating the production personnel – particularly the actors – rather than inhibiting them. An actor needs to establish a deep personal connection with her character, to explore the degree of similarity and contrast between them. Remember that, in performance, the character 'borrows' the actor's body and voice, and her mental and emotional processes; this is what is meant when we speak of an actor 'embodying' a character. It is a delicate, subtle process that involves the gradual building of a relationship between actor and character; in writing stage directions, your task is to promote, rather than impose or dictate, the relationship.

The actor needs precision, clarity and economy from the writer. Give a stage direction only when it is absolutely essential, and make it specific rather than general. Avoid telling the actor how to perform a particular action or how to say a line, by using adverbs ('angrily', 'tearfully'). If the character is angry, choose an action that reveals anger; think about how someone who is angry actually sounds – the language they use, the pace of the speech. Consider what it is that he is angry about, and the degree of anger. You could use numbers on a scale of 1-10 to set the precise pitch, and then write a line that delivers that pitch of anger. Adverbs thus become redundant, because the actor will pick up what it is you require from the gesture and the line itself.

The best way to think about stage directions is to ask:

- What do the actor and the designer need to know, in order to understand the dramatic metaphor?
- What would the audience need to see and hear in order to discover it?
- How can those needs best be answered?

Over-writing

When you write the first draft of your play, you will most likely write far too many stage directions and too much dialogue. You should expect that, and not worry about it at that stage. Over-writing is better than under-writing in a first draft, as it's easier to cut and refine than it is to add – adding all too often appears as 'padding'. But be prepared to edit fiercely when you begin rewriting: every word on your page needs to earn its keep. A good theatre script is always lean and muscular. It can be very spare, with minimum amounts of dialogue and movement, or it can be a torrent of language and activity; either way, it will contain enough for its specific needs, and no more.

Figure 14   The studio theatre.

Figure 15   Railway station.

Figure 16   Petrol station.

SCRIPT EXERCISE

Look at Figures 14–16.

- Fig. 14 is a studio theatre, an empty stage space. It has pale walls that can, if required, be covered with black curtains like those that line the upstage wall. The floor is of pale polished wood that can be covered. The seating arrangement is entirely flexible; it could be rearranged to create any form of stage/auditorium configuration required. There are doors all around the space, and on the upper level, through which actors can enter and exit. It is a small, quite intimate space.
- Figs 15 and 16 are two story worlds.
- Fig. 15 is the concourse of Waterloo railway station in London. It is an interior, public space. It is a busy time of day.
- Fig. 16 is the forecourt of a petrol station, an exterior, public space late at night. A lone motorist is filling up his car.

Choose one of the two story worlds, and write a short scene (three to five pages) that takes place in that world. The stage space for which you are writing the scene is Figure 14, the studio theatre.

The scene should contain no dialogue, only stage directions. Other forms of sound, including non-verbal utterances, sounds and music can be used.

If you should find yourself absolutely stuck, you can use up to three short lines of dialogue in the entire scene. But if you can, try to work your way out of the problem without them.

If you feel inclined, you could write both scenes.

COMMENTS

This may well have proved to be the hardest exercise of all. It requires a large leap of imagination to translate the two big public spaces into the intimate space of the studio

121

theatre. It can also be very tricky to create an exterior location, such as Figure 16 depicts. You must consider very carefully what we need to see and hear, to evoke it. Do you need to have a car onstage, for example? (It can be done: *Miss Saigon*, a large-scale musical, had a helicopter land and take off onstage! The studio theatre in Figure 14 has housed an army jeep, but it couldn't be driven onstage. So you have to think about where and how we enter and exit the scene, if you want to use an actual car.)

Did you think about the atmosphere of the world? It's very helpful to think of descriptive adjectives that would characterize the world. Figure 15 might be 'echoing', 'chilly', 'noisy' or 'impersonal'; Figure 16, with its bright lights amid the surrounding darkness, could be 'welcoming', 'safe' or conversely, 'bleak', 'lonely'. Your adjectives can help you select the key sounds or elements of set and properties that would create the world very economically.

Did you find yourself straining to avoid including dialogue? Did you simply have your characters mumbling inaudibly? The key to writing a silent scene is to find a situation in which words have no natural place; this makes the necessary interplay of gesture, movement and other visual and aural elements much easier to find. For example, if your petrol station scene takes us inside the shop, avoiding the need for dialogue is hard; but if the scene focuses on the point of view of someone sitting inside the car, any interchange between the attendant and the driver buying petrol could be enacted though gesture, as it is a peripheral occurrence. The main story would centre on the person in the car.

If you subsequently review the scene, and think about where you might usefully include a very economical use of dialogue, you will probably be surprised to find how striking the juxtaposition between the speech and the surrounding silence becomes. The dialogue is thrown into sharp relief by the contrast.

That is when dialogue and stage directions are at their best, striking sparks from each other.

AFTERWORD

We've reached the end of our explorations. By this point, you have a number of original scenes to your name, a series of experiments with technique and structure. But they are more than this: they carry the sound of your own voice as a playwright, your own distinctive imprint. You may well have created them by working against, rather than with, the grain of our discussions. If so, that is just as valuable. This book has been as much about the process of understanding and shaping yourself as a playwright, as it has been about the shape of plays.

I hope that you have acquired a taste, as well as an analytical eye, for reading and watching other playwrights' work, both in published form, and in production. Every good playwright pushes the envelope of what can be done in theatre, and how it can be done; keep abreast of where the boundaries are being redrawn, on a regular basis.

I hope, too, that as your pleasure in other playwrights' work has extended, so your respect for the skills of the actor, director and designer will also have grown, along with your desire to work with them. It is a grave mistake for a playwright to consider himself automatically in need of 'defending' the play from the production personnel, and it is a miserable experience to undergo, for all concerned. Not every production experience you have will be a good one, but if approached with an open and flexible attitude, there will be many more good experiences than bad.

And joy – the joy and exhilaration of writing itself, and then going into workshop, rehearsal and performance before an audience, is the whole point of writing a play. Occasionally, fortunes and fame are achieved by theatre writers, but it isn't the most lucrative of businesses; it is extremely time- and effort-intensive. So, in the end, those should be a (welcome!) by-product rather than the over-arching goal.

You should write a theatre play because you have something you want to say, and a play is the best – the only – way for you to say it. And you should relish every step of the process.

Once you have worked on it to your own satisfaction, send it to a theatre company to read. There are a number of companies that specialize in developing and producing new writing. They can be found, in the United Kingdom, through publications produced by the Arts Council, or through organizations such as Writernet and the Writers' Guild (who can also give you advice about protecting your copyright in your play). Many of these organizations can be found online, on the World Wide Web, through keyword searches. But you should also be on the lookout for theatre companies who are touring productions in your local area. Many of the new writing producers are small-scale touring companies, and this would be an excellent means of making an initial contact.

And then, whilst you are sending out this play to be read, you should sit down to write another, building upon what you have learned.

INDEX